THE CHALLENGE OF  LOVE

Making Marriage Work

ENRIQUE ROJAS

 Scepter

Original title: *El amor: la gran oportunidad,* Ediciones Temas de Hoy
© Enrique Rojas, 2011

© Linda Edwards 2011, for the translation © Ediciones Planeta Madrid, S.A., 2011.
Ediciones Temas de Hoy is an imprint of Ediciones Planeta Madrid, S.A.

Also copyright © 2021 Scepter Publishers, Inc.

Published by Scepter Publishers, Inc.
info@scepterpublishers.org
www.scepterpublishers.org
800-322-8773
New York

Cover design by Rose Design
Page design and pagination by Rose Design

Cover image credit: Painting by Valery Rybakow, Shutterstock.com.

Library of Congress Control Number: 2021943365

ISBN: 9781594174308 (pbk.)
ISBN: 9781594174315 (eBook)

Printed in the United States of America

Contents

Preface

What is a human being? It is a big question. The human being is a reality composed of body, soul, and psychology. Achieving a good articulation between these three principles housed within it is essential. For Plato, the relationship between the soul and the body is like that of a sailor and his ship. The classics repeated a Latin expression, *sema soma*: the body as the prison of the soul. Descartes, using the phrase *cogito ergo sum* as his starting point, claimed man was a thinking being. The Greeks called man *zoon logikon*: rational animal. In contrast to Cartesian dualism, there is neutral monism, which does not recognize the difference between soul, body, and psychology.

The human being has a body, as animals do, but also has four key notes inside: intelligence, affectivity, will, and spirituality; these clearly differentiate him from the rest of the animal world.

Intelligence is the ability to grasp reality in its complexity and in its connections. Truth is the conformity between reality and thought. There's a theoretical truth and a practical truth.

Affectivity consists of a set of phenomena of a subjective nature, different from pure knowledge. The term refers to an inner change moving between two opposing poles: like-dislike, attraction-rejection, pleasure-displeasure. Here we find four very concrete experiences: feelings, emotions, passions, and motivations. Affectivity's task is to search for beauty, or in other words, balance, or subjective harmony.

The will is the tendency to reach an objective deemed valuable. It's a rational appetite, which propels us toward a goal. Will's task is to search for the good. I will try to narrow this down. What is good? The good is what we each desire. Or to put it another way: that which is capable of quenching man's deepest thirst. In other words, the good is the inclination to one's own plenitude, which means self-realization.

In this way, three key ideas appear: intelligence seeks truth, affectivity seeks harmony, and the will directs itself toward the good.

The fourth characteristic of the human person is spirituality, which means passing from immanence to transcendence, from the natural to the supernatural, discovering something that goes beyond what we see and touch. We go from a horizontal to a vertical vision. It is to discover the deep meaning of life. All philosophy is born on the shores of death.

I am a big fan of classical music: Beethoven, Mozart, Brahms, and Tchaikovsky. When I attend a concert, it impresses me to see the orchestra's members, each playing a specific instrument: the piano, violin, cello, horn, cymbals, or clarinet. Extrapolating this to the realm of personality, these "members" are perception, memory, thought, intelligence, conscience, and so on. And the conductor is you, the person who manages to bring all of it together.

The personality is each person's own and unique seal. It is the set of current and potential patterns of behavior which give rise to a style, a way of being. And three dimensions reside within it: heredity, which comes with that genetic baggage called temperament; *character*, which is forged through education, family, formation, and the first years of life and its influences; and finally, biography, which is our personal history. For this reason, personality consists of a strongly rooted pattern of behavior resting on three legs: inheritance, environment, and biography.

Psychiatrists pierce below psychological surfaces. We descend to the basement of the personality to put things in order and concert. Moreover, today we are able to talk about personality disorders, which are maladjustments in its functioning. Generally these go unnoticed in superficial relationships, while being observed quite clearly in deep relationships such as the family and intimate friendships.

PART I

Laying the Groundwork
for Marriage

CHAPTER 1.

What is Love?

Love Must Be the Foundation of Life

Throughout history, many things have been said about love from multiple points of view: psychological, philosophical, literary, and poetic. Love is a polyhedral notion; many words inhabit it. Plato's *Symposium* describes love as the desire to reproduce in beauty. In Plato's *Republic,* he also says that the human soul is made of three parts: the *rational,* which resides in the head; the *emotional,* which resides in the chest; and the *concupiscent,* which resides in the abdomen.[1] Each of these parts has a different focus: the reflexive part seeks *knowledge* and *wisdom;* the passionate, *success* and *power*; and the concupiscent, *sexual pleasure.* Another important author in the analysis of love is St. Augustine, who declares in his best-known saying: "Love and do what you will."[2] He follows this advice with an enlightened explanation: "If you stop talking, you will stop talking with love; if you shout, you will shout with love; if you correct, you will correct with love; if you forgive, you will

---

1. Another platonic tale illustrating this idea is that of *Phaedrus,* in which is told the myth of the "winged chariot": a beautiful and temperamental horse represents emotions, a bad and ugly one, concupiscence, and the charioteer, the rational soul, who must drive it with balance regardless of the difficulties.

2. St. Augustine, *Sermon on 1 John 4:4–12.*

forgive with love; if love is rooted in you, nothing but love will be your fruit."[3]

In his *Lectures on Aesthetics*, Hegel suggests that love is giving up our self-perception to lose our self in another self. Additionally, Max Scheler, in his famous work *The Nature of Sympathy*, states: "Love is an intentional movement, passing from a lower value to a higher one in which the higher value of the object or person suddenly flashes upon us."[4]

Love makes living possible. Love is our best guide for behavior. I want you, dear reader, to follow this path with all your attention.

Love is at the same time fascinating and ambiguous, exciting and ethereal, decisive and volatile. It always has an alternative interpretation. It is for this reason that a full, all-embracing definition is so difficult to elaborate. Love has multiple manifestations, some of which are so exalted that its ascetic face, its sacrificial component, is often overlooked. Such distortion often has grave consequences. Love cannot be defined by one feature alone because it has too many sides, faces, and edges.

Classic psychiatry described *transitory mental disorder* as the suspension of discernment for a brief period of time, resulting in irrational behavior. For many this is what love is—a sort of transitory madness altering everything, only to lose strength at a later stage, until it eventually disappears. We cannot feel that we are prisoners of love. Love does not enslave us but liberates us, as the Greeks said. But if we have a full understanding of what love is, then living with it or letting it guide our personal life will be easier. The best practice is always based on a good theory. The effort spent in understanding it will not

---

3. St. Augustine, *Sermon on 1 John*.

4. Max Scheler, *Wesen und Formen der Sympathie* (1913); published in English as *The Nature of Sympathy*, trans. Peter Heath (London: Routledge and K. Paul, 1954).

have been in vain; it will give us clear guidelines as to how to manage our love.

While there is no happiness without love, love is often the cause of unhappiness when it has a poor foundation. Frustrated love is one of the main causes of suffering in modern times.[5] *Positive love* transforms our personal reality, making it better; *negative love* appears when things do not work within the couple, Animals *gather*. Human beings *find* each other. *Finding* means a threefold experience including space, time, and psychology. Love must be a rewarding encounter in which two people, two realities, mutually offer themselves up and decide to share their lives.

Love is increasingly overused, abused, falsely employed, and manipulated.[6] We use it indiscriminately to refer to any sort of emotional attraction. The word *love* operates in a geographical context, which we can compare to a group of floating and scattered islands strewn about the sea of language. We cannot live without love. Love must not turn into a *terminal illness*, the results of which are the inevitable failure of understanding, the triumph of monotony, and the arrival of the final break-up. I see this pattern in my university students; influenced by what they see and hear around them, many of them do not believe in love except as something short-lived that will, sooner or later, inescapably disappear. They think that it is almost impossible for love to last. It is the law of the jungle: a world with no rules in which mere survival is an achievement.

---

5. We have progressively lost the ability to think globally about life. This causes emotional decline and a troublesome connection between love and the other arguments in life. Plato, Aristotle, Shakespeare, Seneca, Cervantes, and the greatest novelists all coincide in their views of how important love is for life.

6. I see every day the deterioration of the meaning of love. While arguments exist for giving up on the attempt to clarify the meaning of love, they are not strong enough; we must keep trying.

Love is a feeling making life itself possible; it is an essential force encouraging human beings to achieve total motivation. Love deserves a privileged place, as it is a universal, life-changing experience. Love is a rich and complex task, full of subtleties. Today, it can be difficult for love relationships to function, because society is disoriented about the subject and especially because love must be nurtured daily. Otherwise, it fades, it evaporates, it disappears.

Love is the need to emerge from within our inner selves and find another to walk together with, through a shared existence. The word love expresses a collection of meanings needing clarification. In so doing, we will discover its greatness, its depth, its strength, its beauty, and also its demands and the work it involves over time—a work of psychological craftsmanship. We must restore its profundity and mystery. We all want to love and find a long-lasting, strong, solid, and great love, capable of embracing all fields of the human condition.

Love always involves the inclination or tendency toward someone we perceive as valuable, positive, and able to motivate us in the life project within each one of us. The lexicon displays a great wealth of words related to love: tenderness, estimation, predilection, propensity, enthusiasm, rapture, ecstasy, effusion, reverence, and, of course, the magic words "falling in love"— that universal experience with which all true love must begin. When we go out into the world, we encounter a variety of facts, situations, and points of view. We need to have the ability to distinguish between sex and love, between desire and love, and between being attracted to and truly needing another person. Imprecision is common. Because of this confusion, many people walk, lost, without a proper grasp on reality and without knowing which way to turn or what to expect.

In order to discover the answers to these questions, a *theory of love* is required. The ultimate task will be to achieve an *adequate practice of love.* Knowledge and education—that is, knowing about love and having clear ideas about a matter so decisive and fundamental—are essential to guaranteeing a mature love life, because understanding too late is not understanding at all. In other words, failing to understand love and its characteristics correctly is a grave and serious problem; it can have long-term, negative implications, opening severe wounds and creating great suffering, which can last a lifetime. This is unsteady terrain, and we have to learn its most important features so that we do not wander aimlessly or choose the wrong paths.

All notions of love include the tendency to desire the company and the well-being of the loved one. This feature implies the manifestation of our preference for one person, among many choices, as the right one to occupy an important place in our lives. Loving someone expresses our wish to be one with that person. Love and union are two words working in harmony. We must not forget that we cannot love what we do not know.

Love is always personal between two human beings, who need each other and live together, with everything this experience entails. Love gives us focus and determines our lifestyle. Animals group in herds and families for protection, and in their own style manifest certain rational instincts. Computers can "think" and carry out intelligent operations, but only humans can be said to love to the full extent of the concept.

Love is what gives true meaning to life. Human love is an all-encompassing experience, touching the most decisive dimensions and the most trivial events of our everyday life alike. Nothing in this life is as important as love. We cannot make the mistake of interpreting it, however, as nothing more than a sweet draught filling our mouth without any effort on our part to make it true, in order to seek our own good and that of the other.

Information and Education about Love

The purpose of this book is to highlight the importance of love for human life. While we must insist that love is an essential feeling; it cannot be reduced to mere affection because it is formed by multiple components. For love to be successful, we must tend each one. This text aims to demonstrate that many couples fail because the full richness of love's component parts has not been fully understood.

Our society is dominated by haste. Everything goes too fast. Moreover, few people pause to consider why so many relationships fail. If love is the foundation of life, it is necessary to understand it before allowing it excessive and uncritical exaltation. The ability to love must stem from knowing what a lasting and fruitful love needs, as well as the fruits we should expect to reap from it.

If we ask how many people around us have the real ability to love, we see very few. We will also observe that many love stories have no future; a deep examination will reveal their very poor knowledge of such a decisive and central issue.

We live in the "information age," constantly receiving news about the latest events worldwide; their significance is short-lived because our unappeasable hunger for still newer events quickly overshadows them. Although it is important to be well informed about what happens in our own country and world, the truly decisive factor is education, rather than mere knowing. Education implies, among other things, possessing the tools to understand the world's meaning and its constant flow of events.

Something similar happens with love. Information about broken love is plentiful. Many people use the failed love affairs of celebrities as a hobby, a distraction to pass the time, as if they were broken toys. Let us think about how many tabloids and television programs are based on romantic misadventures of insignificant characters, told with a frivolity bordering on the grotesque and the comical. Education for love is something different. My aim in these pages is precisely to offer a clear idea about what *true love* is.

Love is an art, and learning it takes time. It requires knowledge and effort. Passion is needed, but so is patience. It demands ongoing education and dedication. Many truncated loves show how weak their foundations were, like a house of cards blown away by external and internal winds. Regarding feelings, a good education does not consist so much in the discovery and classification of different emotional experiences as in their comprehension. Let us not forget that our first contact with reality is of an emotional sort. The heart goes ahead of the mind; for that reason it is necessary to restore emotional intelligence to its rightful position.

Emotional intelligence

Emotional intelligence is in vogue. This is because it has become clear that emotionless intelligence, without the mixture of a good affective education is very limited.

To educate is to bring out the best in a person. Educating feelings is a task of craftsmanship and psychology. To shepherd the affective world is to submerge ourselves in the oceanography of intimacy. To define is to limit; however, a slew of concepts should be grasped. Feelings are positive or negative moods, which bring us closer or further away from the object of desire before us. There are no neutral feelings. Boredom, which might seem neutral, is very close to melancholy; indifference is very close to contempt.

Emotional education begins with knowing our aptitudes and limitations. If we know that we are shy, we have to struggle to acquire skills in interpersonal communication. If we recognize that we are emotionally unstable, we have to put in place the means to acquire more psychological balance. We must also learn how to express feelings. These have different languages and present a certain versatility, which must be united in a clear concept. Here a rich mosaic presents itself; we must not lose sight of the fact that love is the king of myths and, in the collective imagination, this word is magical, full of strength, and wonderful. We must not forget empathy, the ability to put ourselves in the position of the other and understand what is going through their head and heart.

Mature love requires moving from the charismatic to daily life, let us take a look:

1. Cultivate Verbal language. This is knowing how to express and transmit positive affective facts. "I love you." "I need you." "Forgive me, I know I shouldn't have said that." "I want you to know I value everything you do." "Sometimes I can't find the words to tell you how I feel." This is the magic of the word. We develop the vocabulary with a good use of the dictionary. We strive for a rich, fluid, and creative lexical flow.

2. Nonverbal language. A glance, a smile, a wink, holding the person's hand or waist or caressing their hair—all this shows our involvement with the other. Tenderness is the balm of love. All this reinforces and empowers the spoken word. It elevates it.

3. Epistolary language. Write a short and playful note, putting the instruments of affectivity on paper; this may range from asking for forgiveness to giving thanks or acknowledging a mistake made. Any of these are worthy of a note. Those who

are "sentimentally illiterate" do not understand this and are stupefied by the idea; it seems strange to them.

4. The language of small, positive details. To care for small details is love without an expiration date. And the contrary is also true: the systematic neglect of small details is love's ruin; it takes everything for granted and allows lethal monotony to sweep all else away.

5. Care for the language of celebrations. In relationships that work well, frequent celebrations take place, which recall events, experiences, anniversaries. It is not necessary to stage major events, but rather ones rising above the daily routine and giving a festive and sometimes solemn air to existence. Intentions are one thing and results are another.

6. I will add another note to this inventory: the language of surprising the other with something positive, pleasant. Aaron Beck, a New York psychiatrist, says that all the negative passions—hatred, revenge, resentment—gathered together to defeat love, but they could not. Then routine appeared—silently, hidden, with its slow, stealthy, and devastating gait—and could.[7] Novelty is surprise, a window of fresh air that breaks the monotony of days all too similar to one another. It is the zest of life.

7. Finally, develop from time to time the language of small gifts. It is not a matter of giving big things, but of things which in themselves have little material value, whose significance lies in the way and time they are given. Do not confuse price and value here; we can be deceived by price, but not by the merchandise.

---

7. Aaron T. Beck, *Love Is Never Enough: How Couples Can Overcome Misunderstandings, Resolve Conflicts, and Solve Relationship Problems through Cognitive Therapy* (New York: Harper Perennial, 1989).

These seven suggestions activate emotional intelligence and give it wings. The challenge is to know how to unite head and heart, arguments and feelings.

Emotional facts

Education in love also requires being aware of emotional facts. Each emotional fact will be determined by two elements:

1. Our own personal context: what we are doing, where we are, how the main elements of our lives are going—in other words, our circumstances at a given time, our juncture, which is our exterior scenario.

2. The system through which each of us interprets reality: this system is the architectural soundness of the whole building, our *structure,* which is our interior scenario.

The combination of these two elements produces an alloy of reality and hermeneutics from which emotional reactions arise. For many, love is sex and nothing but sex; for those people it will be difficult to fully grasp the information presented in this text. Love affects all dimensions of human life. If we want to understand how love impregnates personality in all its complexity, we need to start from the right coordinates. This is why I will insist over and over again that love is not only a feeling, but also a decision. We must find the connection between love and the other important factors in life. Many people don't believe in the word "love," which has been greatly discredited by the abuse, falsification, and misuse to which it has been subjected; it is used frivolously and indiscriminately to refer to any sort of romantic feeling.

Bear in mind that love is an inexhaustible topic. The more we say about love, the more remains to be said. Knowing about love kindles our desire to enter its folds and secrets, because its essence reaches into a person's very core. Love is the first and last foundation of the human being. That is why we must trap it inside of us, in order to know it and work at it. Love is the starting point of almost every human project, but our contemporary society knows little about it. There is no such thing as marital crisis, only personal crisis. At the beginning of the twenty-first century, society produces ever-more-fragile human beings, people without solid reference points who do not know which way to turn. In these conditions, it is not surprising that so many relationships fail. For this reason there are an increasing number of emotionally stifled people, who lack even the most basic training in this field.

CHAPTER 2.

Falling in Love

The Essence of Falling in Love

Falling in love is among the most stimulating adventures, upon which human beings can embark. It is an unforgettable experience, especially if the outcome is positive, where each contributing event is later recollected with gusto. What conditions must prevail for falling in love? What is "falling in love"? How can we define it?

It is an emotional state loaded with the satisfaction of having found a person, who understands us and with whom to share and negotiate all the experiences that life brings. Falling in love is one form of love—not just any form, but rather the most sublime that humans can experience on a natural level. Contrary to popular myth, falling in love takes place in stages.

As a rule, falling in love is not reached suddenly, unless we are speaking of love at first sight, which is akin to a sudden revelation, instantaneously enlightening one's life with the discovery of a person, who seems to be the right one. It is the encounter of a man and a woman, who stop to stare at one another and, while staring, ask themselves if they could share their lives with that other.

But how do we reach the state of being in love? Are there any previous conditions required? Does everybody fall in love more or less in the same way? Are there fixed rules? Is it always based on the same premises? Two basic factors predispose us to falling in love:

- Admiration: The discovery in the other person of certain features, which we hold valuable, for example a particular lifestyle, the ability to have overcome hardships, an admirable biography deeply marked by exemplary feats, and so forth. Admiration is the capacity to feel awed by somebody else, to believe that person to be worthy of respect, or to feel that thanks to him or her, our perspectives widen. This is the cultural medium in which falling in love becomes possible.

- Attraction: For men, this normally has a physical dimension; while for women, it has more of a psychological nature.[1] In Western society, we can say that men fall in love through their eyes, while women fall in love through their ears. Men are initially attracted to female exterior beauty. Women are often first struck by male interior beauty, namely by what they hear about him, by what he does, his personality or some other qualities. Women generally know more about feelings than men; as a result their sight focuses more deeply, looking inside instead of stopping at the surface.

Attraction is a strong inclination toward another, toward seeking the other's company and conversation, while trying to get to know the other and discover his or her inner self. Physical attraction is followed by a psychological inclination, later to be substituted by a spiritual or cultural attraction, if the spiritual

---

1. Man is more primeval, elementary, and basic. Woman is more secondary, complex, and elevated.

world of the person in love is poorly developed or altogether lacking. These three stages create an essential personal map, which determines the sequence of the steps a person will take in the process of falling in love.

Exterior beauty is easy to grasp. It is right there to be seen. It takes no effort. In order to appreciate interior beauty, on the other hand, we need to pierce the other person's surface, dive into their interior and discover the hidden virtues: harmony, balance, coherence, internal order, joy, and other positive features, which encourage us to explore even further into these territories. Some exterior signal compels and forces us to try to discover what lies inside. Interior beauty is a state of contentment, a well-balanced personality, a private aesthetic.

Physical beauty resides essentially in the face. The whole body depends on the face. There is a popular saying in Spanish that goes, "The face is the mirror of the soul." The face reflects the landscapes of the soul. That is why it is the focal point of the body.

Let us now consider three different aspects regarding why this is the case:

- The first is the face as a whole, which strikes us with its harmony and that somewhat fleeting impression of something aesthetically precise and imprecise, neat and diffuse, tangible and evanescent, all at the same time.
- The second is the eyes, which are particularly important, having their own alphabet. The eyes speak and betray our thoughts, expressing agreement or disagreement. Nothing in the face makes us fall in love as much as the eyes. We are all familiar with the experience of being enchanted by a pair of attractive eyes; their magnetic effect compels us to look at them over and over again. In the first stages of falling in love, the eyes are extremely important.

- Finally, the mouth gains importance through the lips, the laugh, the smile, the serious and thoughtful attitude, the witty word. The mouth is the source of one of the most important issues, communication. Female exterior beauty has an ethereal nature; it is diffuse, imprecise, as though it were just about to fly to who knows where. The person falling in love takes in the loved one's face, making it his or her own. The eyes become the center of attention, because it is in them that the main aspects of facial expressions lie.

These two variables—admiration and attraction—are *sine qua non* conditions for falling in love. They feed on each other. Later, in weeks or months, some other manifestations will emerge. What are they? Let us explore them step by step.

One of the most remarkable is what we could call a certain disruption of attention. Attention is the psychological faculty of focusing our psyche in one specific direction, wherein we concentrate our brain power on some particular issue. It is like a ray of light centering on a particular subject, ignoring all around it. Attention is concentration. Thus our mind becomes absorbed in such a way that both brain and heart are constantly filled with thoughts of the loved one. There are several relevant texts. In his work *On Love,*[2] the Spanish writer José Ortega y Gasset says that people in love suffer from a lack of focus, that they put all other matters aside, and that in such circumstances everything else turns into a blur and reality loses its contours. In normal conditions, attention is spread over multiple objects in our environment, and it focuses on one or the other in a changing pattern.

---

2. José Ortega y Gasset, *Estudios sobre el amor* (Madrid: Revista de Occidente, 1955); published in English as *On Love: Aspects on a Single Theme*, trans. Toby Talbot (New York: World Publishing, 1957).

Here, the opposite phenomenon is at play. This phenomenon that Ortega mentions manifests itself in two ways: to be absorbed by someone and to be charmed by someone. The former facet is intellectual and the latter emotional. To be charmed by someone is to be happy and content when we are with that person: talking, sharing experiences, looking each other in the eye, and seeing life in the same way. In those moments, everything quiets, the world seems to come to a stop, and we wish we could make the ephemeral eternal, stop the clock and savor again in our inner self that delicious time. These positive and inebriating feelings create the foundation on which, little by little, relationships are built.

To fall in love is to find ourselves outside ourselves, that is, to find someone who completes us. In order to define this unforgettable and hopeful experience, the whole sequence of preceding steps needs to be explained.

Falling in Love is the Wish to be Together

The process of falling in love follows several steps. If fully achieved, this sequence will give way to an unforgettable experience. It creates an everlasting mark on a person. Almost immediately, the imperious wish to be together arises. This happens as a consequence of the processes explained in the last section. Afterwards, different ways to manifest our feelings emerge: caresses, kisses, serene silences, intimate dialogues, shared words and private languages, made of a *sui generis* vocabulary understood only by the lovers. It is a subliminal and precious language, full of nuances and the memories of specific moments with special significance for each lover.

Being in love is a desire to have the other person to the exclusion of others, without intermediaries. You and I are enough. I need you next to me, we tell each other. I don't want anyone else here because you are the center of my life. You have moved into the core of my personal world; you are the axis around which I turn.

Being in love progressively gives way to a sense of belonging: you are my life, you are my love, and I need to be next to you. In this stage, exclusivity becomes exalted: I don't want to share you with anybody else. As we can see, the expression of desires springing from these circumstances is of a very specific kind: to be in love is to wish that the ephemeral become eternal, that this experience that we are living will last forever, will remain unchanged, will leave a permanent trace so we can savor these moments of affection and tenderness forevermore. I stop the clock.

Courtship

This is a classic theme for novelists. Courtship implies an ambivalent game in which the lover-to-be approaches and retreats alternately, simultaneously showing interest and indifference. It is an exercise of reciprocal exploration fueled by mutual attraction. The aim is to get to know the other person, to ascertain how he or she really is inside. It is among the most exciting experiences in existence. Feints, maneuvers and strategies are interwoven in a net full of surprises and unexpected turns. At this stage, love hasn't yet materialized.

Seduction is a mechanism with which we attract and compel someone toward us; it often has more to do with appearances than with reality. It is a challenging pastime, very much like a playful, mischievous competition without rules, where alliances and estrangements counteract each other through words, gestures, movements, and verbal and non-verbal words and actions—in short, flirting. The art of seduction rests on an ambiguous foundation, and therein lies a portion of its worth;

ambivalence forces us to ask ourselves whether the other person feels attracted to us. This lack of clarity encourages further and deeper exploration.

All romantic courtship implies a certain love of risk, crowned with the success of a well-handled psychological technique. The apotheosis of appearances gives room to a more and more honest encounter in which the truth of each lover begins to surface. Seduction is a pagan game; love is principally a Christian phenomenon. While seduction plays with the exterior, love encompasses both interior and exterior.

This initial contact provokes a flood of emotional manifestations, progressing from admiration and attraction to feelings of real interest, where we notice all the things we have in common and we seek out the other person's company and conversation. A very important symptom occurs along with this process: we begin to think constantly about the other person, establishing a sort of interior monologue in which we ask ourselves where he or she might be, what he or she might be doing, and say things such things as: "When we see each other again, I want to talk about this or that subject."[3]

In this regard, several points bear mentioning. Ortega says that love is a disruption of attention, because attention goes in only one direction. The nineteenth-century French novelist Stendhal, in his work *On Love*,[4] uses the term crystallization,

---

3. The main character in Cervantes' *Don Quixote* calls Dulcinea, his platonic love, "the lady of my thoughts." To think constantly about a person for whom we feel admiration and attraction means that we are falling in love. It is a revealing fact, and it is important to dwell on it.

4. Henry Beyle Stendhal, *On Love*, trans. Philip Sidney Woolf and Cecil N. Sidney Woolf (New York: Brentano's, 1916). Originally published in French as *De l'amour* in 1822, this is a classic text, translated into many languages.

explained as follows: if we go to the mines in Salzburg, Austria, and drop a stick, in several days the stick is covered in little crystals. Stendhal extrapolates this physical phenomenon to the emotional world: to fall in love is like this crystallization, like idealizing someone, attaching to them more positive values than he or she really has, in a natural reaction to our very human craving for love. I don't fall in love with a real person, but with an ideal. We must remember that this is perfectly normal and that, in due time, things will regain their real shape. In the work of the Italian sociologist Franceso Alberoni, *Innamoramento e amore*,[5] he talks about falling in love as a state of fascination, which illuminates the personal point of view and fills the person with a special strength. Other authors talk about enthusiasm, defined as exaltation, overflowing happiness, exultant affectivity (see for example, Lord Byron, André Maurois, and Somerset Maugham). I have referred to it as a revelation, having the ability to clarify many things, both past and present.

From this point, a couple will take gradual and undefined steps, which will evolve into several phases, and can be defined as follows. On the one hand, the desire to be with the other person is a clear drive toward them and, at the same time, a sensation of time as accelerated.[7] Hours fly and all the time we spend with that person seems short; the clock seems to accelerate, producing

---

5. Francesco Alberoni, *Innamoramento e amore* (Milan: Garzanti, 1979).

6. André Maurois, *Sentiments et coutumes* (Paris: Grasset, 1934); W. Somerset Maugham, *The Razor's Edge* (London: Heinemann, 1941).

7. There are several types of time: the *physical,* marked by the hands of the clock, which cannot be modified in any way; and the *psychological,* which is our own private, personal, and subjective perception of time's passing. Psychological time is an indicator of whether we are at ease and enjoying a particular experience. This distinction is also expressed in the Greek terms *kronos* and *kairos:* the chronological and the private, the legal, and the sentimental.

at the same time a unique feeling of happiness. I believe this manifestation to be of the utmost importance, for it reveals that the process of falling in love advances at a determined, consistent pace, steadily gaining ground.

The Greeks believed that "we cannot love what we do not know." It was a basic premise. In relationships between a man and a woman, this reciprocal knowledge converts the other's qualities into a form of bait. It is a stimulant trip—to conquer and be conquered. In this sense the variety of manifestations is such that a full display would be impossible to grasp. Regarding this, Josef Pieper[8] says, "How wonderful it is that you exist! How lucky I am to have found you on my way!"

---

8. Josef Pieper's essays in *The Four Cardinal Virtues* (Notre Dame, Ind: University of Notre Dame Press, 1965) are truly exceptional and full of wise suggestions.

Chapter 3.

When Is Love True?

Throughout these pages I have tried to dive into love's many nuances, landscapes, and passages. Love is a never-ending theme. Love, together with work, are the two great arguments of life. Happiness consists in being happy with ourselves when we realize that our personal project is working and that we have achieved a mature or balanced personality.

How easy it is to make a mistake in love! When we are young, lacking experience and a long-term vision, serious difficulties revealing our shortcomings appear relatively soon. As previously noted, a man falls in love by sight and a woman by hearing. Between the two ways of falling in love, there are many intermediate arrangements. The step of going out with someone in whom we discover a certain interest implies a gradual psychological exploration, although we are not conscious of it. A study of eighty-four couples, married for more than five years with a positive outlook,[1] showed the following:

- True love brings out the best in you. In those moments, the positivity of what is being lived is such that there is an inner work mobilizing one's best.

---

1. Now is not the time to describe the statistical work and tests used to quantify that the relationship was working well between those couples.

23

- This person helps you grow as a human being. This is an inner, subjective experience, which in my years of dealing with so many people appears quite clearly.

- This person makes me more human. If I was distant, I become closer; if I was cold, I become warmer; and if I had the tendency to treat others harshly, I become softer. A change takes place in the perception of reality and the human environment.

- Love closes past wounds. They move into the background. Psychological maturity can be considered, among other things, as living situated in the present, trying to get the most out of it; reconciled with the past, I can live open to the *future*.

- Chronological time seems to accelerate. When we are falling in love, time flies; it goes very fast; and we spend hours together almost without realizing it. This is a very significant symptom.[2] We feel good; we're comfortable, and in tune. I have even heard this type of person say more than once, "When I am with her, there seems to be no time for anything . . . it's dizzying."

- If this love is true, solid, and authentic, what we want is to make the other person happy, to use all means to give them the best,[3] and to make them feel good, happy, and at ease. Our own happiness gives way to doing everything possible to contribute to the other person's happiness.

---

2. In depressive patients, the experience of chronological time is that time does not circulate—it has stopped—and they look again and again at the clock, with a feeling of anxiety mixed with boredom. On the other hand, in euphoric patients, the experience is the opposite: everything is fast.

3. In superficial affective relationships, where we seek ourselves and where there is a panic of commitment, this does not happen—nor when what someone seeks is sex pretending to be love.

- An interesting idea appears: life is inconceivable without that person at my side. In other words, you are part of me, and my life has no meaning without you. This is falling in love. Telling the other person, I need you.

Those who are full of themselves do not need anyone. Being satisfied with ourselves makes it is difficult to have an authentic love. This is seen quite often in the person of today.[4] In true love, everything inclines towards the affirmation of the other, ahead of ourselves.

Authentic love begins as a feeling; then it becomes an act of both the will and intelligence. Feeling, will, and intelligence combine with a fourth element, spirituality, which gives height, density, and cohesion to the previous three.

---

4. It is what I have called the commitment panic syndrome, which is a complex mixture of fear, rejection, and firm resistance to telling the other person "I love you," because if I do I lose my freedom and I must be involved with you in the future.

CHAPTER 4

Making the Right Choice

Love and Knowledge

When two people know each other well and complement one another, a psychological summit is reached: the sudden realization that they have found what they were seeking. No other encounter is so decisive; this realization changes the direction of our personal life. From this point, our personal life assumes a well-defined, specific direction.

This epiphany reveals to us the other person, who occupies both our interior and our exterior space. The romantic revelation is an extraordinary experience, which brings the promise of virility and strength; it is present and future happiness. During the process of falling in love, the other becomes our other half. In the first stages of falling in love, a certain element of irrationality exists; our tendency towards the other person works as a sort of magnet pulling us in their direction.[1]

Women make men more human, and also more spiritual. Men provide women with security.[2] At this stage, love has

---

1. This is similar to St. Paul's falling off his horse on his way to Damascus. He is blinded, but it changes his life. Suddenly, he has discovered the love of his life.

2. Women are embracing; men are invasive. Women let men embrace and support them. Men insist on embracing women; women are more welcoming. At the psychological level, women want to be understood and men want to be valued.

already appeared; its arrival has an ennobling influence. What were previously only ideas and interpretations of life, become shared experiences placing the other person in the center of our individual universe. To fall in love is to create a private mythology, which we share with someone. In this way, we make the selection of the loved one with whom we want to share our lives. This choice has a threefold meaning: I am going toward you; I am going with you; and you are my project. These meanings can be summarized in the ultimate statement: *you are my life.*

You are my future, my ambition, my goal, where I am going, and the place toward which all my hopes are directed; you give my life its primary purpose.[3] You are the script of my life and its main plot. Our trajectories cross. We are each the principal purpose of the other.

Love, being in love, and knowledge: these three areas of emotional exploration form an interconnected system. This is the flame of love. According to the *Oxford English Dictionary,* a flame is "a hot glowing body." Love is the original fire from which the glowing body of falling in love arises. They support and feed each other; all the while being fanned by yet another vital flame, that of knowledge. In a few words: love and knowledge are the two flames of personal life.

Making the right choice is the key. There is nothing like love to reflect the truth behind every person. Once the initial feelings of drunkenness and overexcitement pass, we must be able to value the real worth of the other person. Female beauty has been the perdition of many men; the power of a beautiful woman is such that it pulls men like a magnet. Often, they forget to value her real worth, wondering whether behind that beauty lies the ideal person to complement them.

---

3. Happiness involves hope. Hope is not the content of happiness, but its trappings. We live in a present steeped in future expectations, full of good omens.

Choosing the Right Person

Many people never ask themselves how they should go about choosing the right person; however, it is of vital importance. Many people err and do not make the right choice.

Sometimes love appears suddenly, decidedly, and unexpectedly. At other times, love is sought after zealously; we keep our eyes wide open as we meet new people so as not to miss any opportunity, which may present itself. Women look for a deeper relationship, with the ultimate aim of building a home and having children. On the other hand, men are different, tending to look for more superficial relationships without further implications.[4] For this reason, it is important to develop an approximate male or female model of what we are looking for in order to possess a reference point. We have to put in the preliminary work of deciding the preferences, styles, and contents we want and expect to attain.

The choice consists in selecting from a certain human prototype, and profile. As said in the first chapter, this can be divided into four main features: physical, psychological, cultural, and spiritual. At first, the physical aspect is paramount and is the logical course of events. We make our first impression through our physical aspect; our body and face together reflect our personhood. Physical attraction is fundamental; if it did not exist and only the psychological aspect operated, the foundations of love would fail.

True love is selective. It has to be. If love takes shape and gains stability, it determines nothing more and nothing less than the person with whom we will join to become an *us*.

---

4. I must press two points in this stage of our voyage across the emotional seas. First, it is now common for men to give a pretension of love in order to obtain sex, and for women to give a pretension of sex in order to obtain love. Second, it is common for men and women over thirty years of age to suffer the panic of commitment syndrome. Commitment is a frightening thing and we run away from it.

Love's remaining components are equally important. The psychological dimension consists of the compatibility of personalities, the agreement of two lifestyles, the evaluation of the possibility of good communication, and so on (see chapter 6 below). The cultural facet also has an equally notable role, although it may appear at first to be of secondary importance. It is critical for the two parties involved to have a similar cultural perspective and to manifest an equal wish to grow in that direction. The spiritual dimension is crucially important; thus it is essential that it be considered from the beginning of the relationship. If spiritual discussion remains superficial, it is possible that this issue will not even be recognized, either because one of the parties has no beliefs or because neither dares to bring it up. Neglecting the spiritual is a gross mistake; sharing ideas and values and living them with simplicity, coherence, and valor are one of the couple's most solid foundations. In our excessively secular society, it can be difficult to discuss the spiritual, but it nevertheless needs to be addressed.

The profile of the other person thus becomes clear. This is necessary to keep ourselves from being carried away by the whirling current of the passion of the first moments. Intelligent love consists of heart, mind, culture, feelings, reason, and spirituality. If this combination is neglected, the later results can be disastrous. Love may be blind when it arrives, but it will certainly be prescient when it leaves. In the midst of the intoxication of falling in love, we must be responsible enough to evaluate the advisability of moving forward with the relationship.

I must stress how uncommon this balanced and prudent evaluation of a selection is in modern times. Allow me to explain. Things often happen in such a way that people get caught up in the emotional tide and either cannot or do not know how to pause to consider the future prospects of the relationship. On these occasions, events adopt a rapid, impulsive, frenetic pace.

The attraction is so overwhelming that an appropriate use of reason is not possible without the emerging love losing some of its freshness. The intellectual face of love is not very popular, but it is immensely valuable as the real foundation for the future success of the relationship. Some might argue that an excess of analysis can kill the spontaneity of those moments, but I believe that it is preferable to apply such reason right at the beginning, before we find our emotions prisoner to the other person, making it much more difficult to change the situation or end the relationship.

Love without selection often leads to serious mistakes and erroneous expectations. That is why it is so important to realize when our guidelines are poorly designed and their foundations badly laid. In these cases, the wise course of action is to abandon the relationship and start looking for somebody else.[5] Don Quixote famously says, "He who chooses well in marriage, has nothing left in which to choose well." The next step is protecting this love, nourishing it, and kindling it as a fire in the hearth. Looking after the small details keeps love alive. At first, the arrival of love disturbs our life, turns it upside down, and confronts it with itself. Later, it organizes it, lending it strength and stability, and constructing the foundations of a common building of solid architecture.

---

5. My experience as a psychiatrist has allowed me to witness many couples splitting up because their relationships were built on demolition debris, with no consistency. In these cases, it is easy to predict that a collapse will occur sooner or later. For example, couples seeing each other for a long time and having frequent discussions, in which harsh words and disqualifying names are exchanged, usually do not have a good prognosis. This is also the case with couples, who have broken up many times and later resumed the relationship. If this pattern establishes itself before marriage, things usually continue along the same path after the wedding. My experience compels me to advise these people to end the relationship. In these cases, some degree of realism based on practice is advisable. The intervention of a psychologist, psychiatrist, or counselor may be of use.

CHAPTER 5.

Seven Tips Before Marriage

Necessary Warnings

The language of love is at once solemn and playful. Deciphering the rich vocabulary of love requires the patience of a botanist, an archaeologist, or a medieval monk copying a manuscript. Words weave a dense net of meaning; it is therefore important not to get lost in the maze of words and meanings. Love must be our natural habitat, our basic ecological niche.

It is surprising that such an important issue, in which so many hopes and expectations are placed, can end up badly over and over again. In any other field of knowledge, such as medicine, engineering, or physics, any mistake or anomaly is analyzed in depth until the source or cause of the malfunction is discovered. In the human sciences, the same measures are not often taken. It is very sad to see so many broken couples around us; yet, the only responses normally evoked seem to be regret and, afterwards, skepticism.

Consequently, we must examine the reasons behind so many fiascos and analyze the nature of love. The art of married love is comprised of theory, practice, and ongoing learning. This threefold structure summarizes the main features of that lasting love, desired by so many but achieved by so few. In order to learn the art of love, good knowledge regarding the nature of both personhood and love is mandatory. As a rule, however, love is not studied while we are young and begin seeing other people.[1]

To those about to embark on the adventure of married love and to those who have made the decision to join their lives in any way,[2] I wish to give seven pieces of practical advice. I accompany each suggestion with a clinical example, personally documented by myself and my team, which I believe useful for the explanation of those ideas.

1. Don't Idealize Love

Love is often exalted in classic and popular songs, infecting the spirit of young people, who become intoxicated with the term, converting it into something magical, wonderful, and excellent. This exaltation is a mistake. Literature, poetry, and romantic music exalt love to such a high pedestal that when the real experience does arrive, the obstacles make it fall short of expectations. The love between a couple is real and has defined coordinates; while being strong, its strength depends on the care and effort with which each party tends it.

---

1. It may be that this phenomenon receives more attention today as a consequence of the epidemic of ruptures, but certainly not as much as is desirable. While the major collective maladies of the last century have been analyzed rigorously and in detail, no such investigation has occurred in the field of love. There is ample evidence for that.

2. For Catholics, this joining should take place within the sacrament of matrimony. This sacrament is a sacred act, which conveys the Grace to raise the union from the natural to the supernatural and the immanent to the transcendent.

Clinical case 1

A man, thirty-five, married his girlfriend after dating her for eighteen months. He is an engineer, with two siblings. He has always been a rather shy, reserved, and uncommunicative person, very attached to his mother. In this sense, it can be said that his dependence on his mother is pathological. The death of his father, when the son was twenty-two, is noteworthy.

At thirty, he had another girlfriend, of whom he says: "I left her on my mother's advice. I liked her, but my mother said that she was not the right girl for me, that she was very domineering with too strong a personality."

And he proceeds: "I thought that love was the most wonderful thing in the world and that the day I fell in love with someone I'd marry her. Although I am quite shy, in the last few years I have managed to open up a bit. I met my girlfriend one summer and was very attracted to her from the start; I saw that she was open with people, very communicative and at ease in interpersonal relationships; those qualities complement mine. Our beliefs were very different. I am very religious—I was raised that way—but she was barely religious at all. She always said that the important thing was not to do harm to others and to walk your own path without hurting anyone. . . . That difference made me doubt; while neither my siblings nor my mother liked it, I ultimately said, love will sort things out.

"She tended to argue, which is something that didn't sit well with me. I have always been a very calm person; I realized that we were fighting over things of no importance, ridiculous rows that invariably ended badly. . . . I thought that once we were married this would change, because love conquers all.

CONTINUED

33

Clinical case 1 CONTINUED

"I had never read anything about feelings and always thought the subject of little interest to me. We got married; I soon realized how difficult it was to live with another person. We argued a lot and it affected us both, especially me. I used to go three or four days without talking to her, going over and over the things she had said. I opted to choose my words carefully, being very careful about what I said. Being on guard all the time was very difficult for me. Because of these problems we went to a psychologist for couples therapy, which is the last thing I had ever imagined I'd need. The psychologist told me two things: firstly, that I was hypersensitive in my relationship with my wife, that I let everything affect me too much, and that I needed to try to change that; and secondly, that I suffered, in current psychological terminology, from *alexithymia*,[3] a word that I had never heard before and that literally meant that I had an incapacity or severe difficulty in expressing my feelings. In other words, I could not formulate nice things to tell her, ways to compliment her . . . and the truth is that I recognized myself in both cases.

"My mother told my wife three things needing correction on her part: her impulsiveness, her tendency to argue over incidentals, and her habit of bringing up the laundry list of past mistakes.

CONTINUED

---

3. An emotionally stifled person is called an alexithymic, which is defined as a person with a deficiency in understanding, processing, or describing emotions. This condition almost always appears in men and very seldom in women. This kind of man only becomes affectionate minutes before conjugal relations, producing a logical reaction of anger in the woman.

Clinical case 1 CONTINUED

"We started this therapy a year after we got married. Every time we went, I had a bad time because I had the impression that I was on the examination table. It was too much for me and I couldn't improve. I had an idealized notion of love, maybe because of all those popular songs; I've always considered myself a romantic. . . . Finally, two and a half years after getting married, we decided to separate. It was just too difficult to be together due to constant arguments; days without talking to each other and the intervention of her family, pointing out yet more things I did wrong—it was all very sad."

When our team first met this couple, they were already separated. He came with his mother and one brother to see if anything could be done to rescue his marriage. We contacted his wife and invited her to see us, so we could work with both of them and hear all sides of the story. She came only once; she did so to tell us a list of grievances against her husband. Nothing could be done, despite their desire to try and in spite of the fact that he was an active Catholic. He had told me, "I'll do anything I can to save my marriage. I was married by the Church and I know what that means."

Our study determined that he suffers from a personality disorder with three very significant features: excessive dependence on his mother, excessive shyness (modern diagnostic criteria refer to this as avoidant personality disorder), and emotional immaturity. Added to this, of course, is an idyllic view of love, more typical of teenagers than of grown men.

2. Don't Idolize the Other

Avoid overvaluing the person you have chosen. During the initial stages of being in love, idealizing the new loved one is normal, but as months go by it is necessary to begin to see the other in reality, by honestly assessing his or her virtues and defects. In the initial stages of falling in love, it is difficult to make a sufficiently objective evaluation; such a vision emerges bit by bit, but it does eventually develop. The clarity this vision provides allows us to analyze the reasons why we fell in love and how the sequence of events developed. In the previous chapter we mentioned Stendhal's crystallization,[4] Ortega's attention disorder, Alberoni's nascent state, and our shared private mythology. Each of these feelings offers a different perspective on the beauty and profundity of the emotionally charged circumstances of the first stages of being in love. We must, however, try to avoid "losing our head," in a figurative sense, over the other person. If this idealized view is not corrected after some time, the relationship will inevitably deteriorate into a difficult experience, with all sorts of conflicts just around the corner.

Clinical case 2

The next case involves a woman, twenty-six. She maintains social relationships and works for a fashion magazine. She is upper-middle-class, but with limited education. She studied

CONTINUED

---

4. Marcel Proust makes some interesting remarks based on Stendhal's theory: perfections found by the lover in the loved one sprout from qualities missing in himself and that, in a way, would *complete him as a person*. That is why very different people initially attract one other. These adornments that the lover sees in his beloved, however, can materialize in reality, if love develops harmoniously.

Clinical case 2 CONTINUED

design for one year in a private school and then found her job through her mother.

She tells us her story: "I had my first boyfriend when I was seventeen and he was twenty-four. It lasted for three years. At first, everything was wonderful; he seduced me. I was very inexperienced because of my age, while he had already had several girlfriends. Handsome, tall, and very good-looking, he was noticed by everyone and many girls more or less my age went after him. Therefore, it was such a surprise that he set his sights on me. At first I couldn't believe it; additionally, he had already finished his law degree and was working for a small legal firm, which was very attractive to me. My parents were not very happy about it because I was so young and he completely dominated me. Since he was seven years older, his personality was overwhelming."

She proceeds: "I started studying several things, but I've never liked books. I went from studying art and interior design to doing languages (English and French). Little by little, I let it go until I was only studying English, which was easier for me; I never worked at it enough. Later, a friend encouraged me to take some courses in public relations, which I did enjoy since the lessons seemed to stay naturally in my head without my having to study much.

"I realized that not having completed a university degree made me feel frustrated and left me with a bit of an inferiority complex. I started to feel jealous of my boyfriend, who had an active social life because he had many friends. I considered him an idol; I thought that any of my female friends

CONTINUED

37

would be happy to have a man like him. I started thinking that I could lose him . . . and after some months, the idea that the best thing was to get married took over me. I suggested it to him and, at first, he reacted very badly. He said that despite his having a stable job and good salary, it would be best to wait awhile. I took it badly. After several weeks of great tension, he decided to end the relationship. I was devastated; I used to spend all day in bed, crying and turning over all that had happened in my head. My mother, without my knowledge, called him and talked to him. He called me again and I couldn't believe it; I could still get back the man of my life, my idol of a boyfriend! At the beginning, I did not dare to speak about getting married, but the issue soon reappeared and my mother intervened again. Thanks to her cunning, we finally got married. A couple of weeks before the wedding, I chanced to hear that he had been going out with two girls. The news left me devastated. I never told him. I was afraid that he'd leave me again, but he noticed that something was wrong; he insinuated that if I wanted, we could put off the wedding or even end the relationship altogether. This so utterly destroyed me that my mother took me to a psychiatrist, who gave me some medicine for my nerves, telling me that everything would be fine.

"We got married. After a few months, I realized I had made a mistake. I had thought that he was an exceptional man—I remembered how successful he was with women, his ability for social relationships, and how handsome he was. . . . But after a short time, I realized that he was

CONTINUED

Clinical case 2 CONTINUED

very selfish; he always did what he wanted, never thought about me, and he spent all day working, constantly attending meetings. More than anything, I realized that the idol I believed him to be had completely disappeared and that, at home, he was even vulgar. Our sex life wasn't very good; I needed him to put me in the right psychological mood with tender words—I don't know, I think every woman likes that—but he always said he was tired, that he worked long hours, and that for him sex was very important. . . . We went on like this, the relationship deteriorated, and we moved further and further away from one another as time went by. I noticed that I had stopped admiring him; that was a big deal to me. I also noticed that he didn't respect my work because I earned much less than he did. He used to throw in my face that he supported us economically and that I didn't contribute much. . . . That's how the insults started. His close friend, also a lawyer but in a different firm, had recently divorced his wife. He told my husband all about his marriage troubles and that he had decided to split up."

She then goes on to comment on the negative influence that friend had had on her relationship, since his advice was simply to separate if things didn't work. "That advice greatly affected me and I didn't know how to handle the situation. . . . My mother, who got along quite well with my husband, intervened yet again and put us in touch with a priest. It was the best thing that happened to us; he was forty-one, a doctor, very sound, and understanding of us from the beginning. He set up behavioral patterns for us to follow and

CONTINUED

helped draw us closer to God. My husband had neglected his spiritual side, but I was still strong in that regard, due to formation from both school and at home. Things improved steadily.

"The priest told me: 'You have made two mistakes in your marriage because of your age and you must consider them carefully: 1) you had made your husband an idol, however everyday life grounds us in reality; living together is a skill needing to be learned; and 2) spiritual life is crucial for married life; ignoring this truth is like having a large library at home and not using it.' For me, his arguments were definitive. Everything has changed for the better; I realize my mistakes and the things, which we have both done wrong. We now want to turn our life around."

I kept in touch and have continued to monitor the situation. The intervention of this priest occurred about a year after the wedding, when the relationship was at its lowest point. Later, I was able to talk to both husband and wife; the relationship had changed drastically. Both attend family orientation courses and have started helping other troubled couples. He has taken his commitment to work less seriously. She has had her first child and is expecting a second.

3. Being in Love Does Not Guarantee Long-Term Success

How easy it is to fall in love and how difficult to stay in love. This is the psychological arena in which we have to work. How do we keep love alive? Looking after the small details makes love strong, firm, and well-founded. Conversely, we can say that systematically neglecting the small things destroys love. Without constant care, passion cools down and the relationship progressively deteriorates. Gradually, the two parties grow apart. We must act and take the necessary measure to prevent such distance from developing.[5]

Everyday life is not trivial or insignificant; it cannot be neglected. In these small details, there is an uncultivated field needing to be explored and toiled in. A sensible man should ask himself: "What can I do to make my wife happy? What small thing can I do to make her feel good? What does she expect from me?" Whoever thinks that these things are silly and unimportant knows very little about nourishing love. The theory of love is one of the three pillars where the art of love rests.

Clinical case 3

This case involves a forty-two-year-old doctor, who married a thirty-six-year-old nurse after they met at the hospital where they both worked. Married for twelve years, they have three children. He experienced the violent separation of his parents, physical and psychological abuse, severe

CONTINUED

---

5. I often hear patients or others say, "I have fallen out of love; it's gone; I don't feel what I used to anymore." Before we reach this situation, there are plenty of alternatives. Think about how much effort people invest to improve their professional situation, to earn more money, to be more successful, or to ascend some steps in the social ladder. We should do at least as much for our married lives. We must look after these things, instead of neglecting them, and try to restore the freshness of the first days.

Clinical case 3 CONTINUED

emotional neglect on his father's part, and poverty. Of his three siblings, two are separated.

He explains: "The more I knew of her, the more attraction I felt; she was affectionate, delicate, very professional, and I was surprised at how little notice she took of me. I think it took her a while to call me by my first name. I remember that one day a patient, who had attempted to commit suicide by ingesting pills, was brought into the ER. He was in awful shape, but miraculously we managed to save his life. As she was working with this patient, I was watching her hands, her eyes, her dedication . . . everything about her exuded love and professionalism. I also thought about my parents' house, in which everything was negative, filled with frequent arguments, shouting, reproaches."

He proceeds, "I had a sort of epiphany, telling myself that this is my ideal woman. I have always been rather shy, insecure, and not very affectionate;[6] I was not very good with the little details because I had not seen them in my parents' house. Dialogue was a problem for me and I was very protective of my privacy. . . . All these thoughts went through my head during the night I found myself transfixed by her.

CONTINUED

---

6. Life is like a boomerang; if you receive love, you will give love, and if you receive hate and aggression, you will end up reacting with aggression and disdain. I have said elsewhere that our childhood determines everything. What happens then, stays with us forever. Imitation and contrast are two opposite kinds of learning processes. The first involves the copy of healthy models present in our environment; the acquisition of imitative behaviors is easier because they reflect what we have seen. The second kind involves doing exactly the opposite of what one has seen, as expressed by this patient, "I have learned to treat women in exactly the opposite way to how my father treated my mother. I turned disdain into tenderness, shouting and threats into gentleness . . . but I have lacked a teacher."

Clinical case 3 CONTINUED

"After several weeks, I managed to change my attitude and started looking for ways to bump into her, as if by coincidence. Even then, I was surprised at how little notice she took and at how she didn't seem to notice that I was after her. I heard that she had a sister, who was a doctor, and another one who was a nurse. I started taking an interest in her life and discreetly finding out things about her.

"We coincided on a shift on New Year's Eve, which is often particularly difficult because people drink too much and lose control. She was also working. After midnight, a few of us were having some champagne in the lounge where we normally went for food or a coffee. There were hugs, well-wishes . . . but I didn't see her. Hours later, I saw her in the ER, attending an intoxicated patient, who had been hit in the face with a bottle and needed fifteen stitches. I wished her a happy New Year; looking me in the eye, she said, 'I wish you the best and may God be always with you.' It was certainly no customary or merely polite "Happy New Year." Encouraged, I said, 'I'd like to take you out for dinner later or tomorrow.' I took the leap from treating her as a colleague to asking her on a date. That is typical of me; one moment I hardly speak to people and the next I am telling them my life's story."

He continues, "I fell in love with her on the first date. We went out for lunch and I was completely captivated with her words, her green eyes, and her elegant and slender hands. She stressed her words with a very special motion of the hands. I did not want lunch time to end; I would have stopped the clock. But what I liked best about her was her

CONTINUED

43

Clinical case 3 CONTINUED

way of thinking; her family was very close and she adored her parents. She was particularly close to her father and a brother. She was religious but not prudish; she was also very cheerful."

Here we see in him the manifestation of the main symptoms of falling in love. She, who is more reflexive and more emotionally mature, took things more slowly. According to them, they got married after a year of going out together. They have been together for twelve years and have three children. Approximately a year ago, the relationship started experiencing difficulties. Our team asked each of them, separately, three basic questions in order to ascertain the status of their relationship:[7]

1. What are the main areas of conflict between you, in order of importance?
2. What would you add or subtract from your personality to improve your relationship?
3. What would you add or subtract from your spouse's personality?

According to her, the main points of conflict are that he is not affectionate or expressive, that he neglects the small things, and that there is a lack of communication between the two. To a lesser degree, she complains about his not helping in the house, spending too much time in front of the computer, and not involving himself enough

CONTINUED

---

7. This is what we call psychological tracking; it gives us complementary information to that obtained by separate, face-to-face, initial interviews.

Clinical case 3 CONTINUED

in raising the children. He, on the other hand, leaves this field blank, because he believes that there is nothing to tell in this regard.[8] I explained his psychological shortcomings to him and gave them both a personalized behavioral program, with a list of very specific rules aimed at reinforcing the positive behaviors of the other. He doesn't want to split up under any circumstance, but at the same time he strongly resists changing very specific aspects of his behavior toward her. She is tired, because the situation has worn her out. Additionally, she has read books on couples psychology and has realized that they need external help to be able to redirect the situation.

After a few sessions of couples therapy, he changed very significantly. His wife says, "My husband needed someone with authority to tell him what to do to win me back, and that some things he does hurt me very much. Now I see how hard he's trying to follow your instructions: he spends more time with me, we talk more, he has started reading stories to the two younger children at night. . . . I think, Dr. Rojas, that my husband did not receive enough love at his parents' house and that influenced many aspects of his personality. Because of your advice, I see that our relationship has embarked on a new, positive journey."

He says: "I thought that, since I was so much in love with my wife when we got married, everything would be fine. I never thought that she could feel bad over those things she

CONTINUED

---

8. In the West, in general, men know less about feelings than women; they don't value them as much and, if they are lacking, they do not miss them. Women are exactly the opposite.

Clinical case 3 CONTINUED

---

has mentioned. I admit that I have neglected them, but the truth is that I gave such things little value. I am willing to change and follow your directions. I have never been affectionate, and you insist that this must be worked out through psychotherapy. I must say that when I was studying medicine, they hardly talked about these things at all and the little they did say, I had almost forgotten."

We have here a very interesting example. When the disposition of both parties is good, with a willingness to change specific things, the prognosis is often positive. In this specific case study, instead of a marital crisis[9] in the strict sense, we should talk about a personal crisis, which ends up affecting the spouse.

---

4. Married Life Requires Constant Learning

Nobody knows everything about the infinite nuances, which can develop between couples. The emotionally immature think that everything will be alright, that there will be no problems, and that difficulties will sort themselves out. However, we must remember that it takes years for a couple to develop a deep

---

9. Every couple, sooner or later, will go through some type of crisis. There is no life without crisis, and when correctly interpreted, crises can and should encourage growth, improve the quality of love, and defeat bitterness and resentfulness, one of love's biggest foes.

Therefore, I believe that talking about crises is something positive—an opportunity to rethink things and turn them around, to negotiate, to yield, to recognize mistakes, and take a common step forward. Crises within a couple are painful, but if both cooperate, it is wonderful to see how the right path can be retaken. Growing in love is a painful experience.

understanding of one another. As the relationship progresses, many unforeseen facets will emerge.

We must take careful note of acts, anecdotes, experiences, and misfortunes, learning to harmonize all the dimensions of love, namely the sexual, psychological, and cultural. In order to achieve harmonious growth, both parties must learn how to balance such factors as the position of the respective families, the economic situation, the free time each party chooses to spend with the other, and so on. Many variables need to be combined.

Clinical case 4

In this case, we will talk about a man, sixty-six, who owns his own legal firm and has many employees. His story is both interesting and sad. Son of a wealthy family, he has amassed a fortune of his own. Currently married to his fourth wife, he summarizes his emotional life as follows:

"I always wanted to be a lawyer. I prepared for a very difficult public examination, but I didn't pass. That was a shock for me, because I had an uncle and a cousin who had passed. Eventually, I realized that I hadn't studied hard enough. Telling people I was studying to be a notary public, fresh out of law school, made a very positive impression on them; it made me highly successful with women. As a university student, I had several girlfriends, nothing serious; I only wanted to have a good time and come and go as I pleased. I abandoned my spiritual side because I started having sex very young. After I failed the public exam, my goal changed and I became obsessed with making money

CONTINUED

Clinical case 4 CONTINUED

Consequently, I was surrounded by people for whom that was the only goal.

"At twenty-nine, I got a girl pregnant. I was forced to marry. Although my parents told me to think it over carefully, her parents were adamant. I married her and soon saw that it was very difficult for me. I was used to doing what I liked and to having no responsibilities; even my university studies took me two years longer than usual to finish, because I took them at my own pace. I was not ready to get married at that age and much less to be responsible for someone else. The relationship was bad and we had frequent arguments. I lived my own life, despite being married, and even had some casual relationships with other women-lawyers working for other firms. My wife never knew, but what it proved is that I didn't love her enough. She was a housewife and spent a lot of time with our son. Eventually, she told me that things would improve if we had another child. We did; however, everything went on pretty much as before. She was a good, pleasant person, but I stopped finding her physically attractive; besides, whenever we argued, she refused to have relations. That infuriated me. Finally, we agreed to separate; I was thirty-six and she was twenty-seven. Everything was done by common agreement. Her father told me two things, which sat very badly with me at the time, although after all these years I have realized how right he was: 'You are immature and you don't know how to treat a real woman.'"

This case is interesting because the patient is emotionally immature and his life is lacking in balance; his only aim is to be professionally successful and make lots of money.

CONTINUED

Clinical case 4 CONTINUED

He proceeds: "I then enjoyed a few great years. I lived in my own apartment and did whatever I wished. I saw my children every now and then, but they were more a burden than an emotional comfort; I saw them because I had to and because my parents insisted on it. I went out with many girls and had lots of sex . . . things went on like this for a few years. Then, when I was forty-two, I met one of the prettiest women I had ever seen. She was twenty-four and a language student, who worked in the public relations department of a large multinational company. I met her at a birthday party and was physically attracted to her from the first moment. It was something similar to being a teenager again. I was eighteen years her senior, but she had a very confident personality. It took me a lot of effort to win her over; neither she nor her family liked the fact that I was divorced.

"After many misadventures, we got married in a civil ceremony. I was forty-four and everything seemed perfect. However, the same old problems reappeared with the daily routine. Even worse, my wife had to travel abroad for professional reasons; I started feeling something I had never felt before, namely jealousy. I had realized that at parties and dinners she got a lot of attention because of her beauty and her personality. It was as though she was overshadowing me. Sometimes we quarreled about it; I went as far as insulting her, which led to more arguments, frowns, and brooding silences. She even went to stay with her parents for a while. I apologized and we resumed our relationship; it was then that she became pregnant. That new hope drew us closer. We had a daughter.

CONTINUED

Clinical case 4 CONTINUED

"It was also then that I started seeing a divorced woman, about twelve years younger than me. I had known her for a long time because she worked in the same firm as my cousin. It was fun at first and tragic in the end, when my wife found out. I denied everything, but several witnesses confirmed the relationship to my wife. In only a few weeks, she was talking about divorce in the most adamant terms. Not wanting to be left behind, I hurried things forward and practically took the initiative. I didn't know that infidelity could be taken so badly by a woman. The divorce was hard; she got a lot of money from me, and, what's more, she hardly let me see our daughter. Those months were very painful, but in the end I told myself: 'You are already fifty and that's life, so live and enjoy yourself without worrying about anything.'

"After that relationship I said to myself: 'Your mistake is that you committed yourself to a woman. Stay as you are, living on your own, and do whatever you want. Focus on your work and make new friends.' I ended up with a group of friends, more or less my age, almost all separated, and devoted to the good life and going out. I told myself, 'Do not fall in love again under any circumstances,' and several years passed like that until I met the woman who would become my third wife. I was fifty-seven at the time. She was a Swedish girl of twenty-seven, another sculptural beauty. She had come to Madrid to study Spanish and was living at my cousin's house. I met her during the summer, when we all went on a weekend holiday. As I have said several times, women win me over with their looks; beauty and youth are enormously

CONTINUED

Clinical case 4 CONTINUED

attractive to me. I forget everything else about that person—her personality, what she has studied, what she does for a living—and besides, sex has always been my foremost interest, which soon followed. I just thought of it as a pastime and a conquest—though, since I was thirty years older than she was, her attention stroked my ego."[10] We went out, traveled together, had sex very often . . . and nothing else. However, she had talked to her parents and friends about me, and I realized she was serious; I only wanted to have a good time and not even consider anything else. When she realized where I stood, she left me, after about two years. I took it well and told myself, 'It's for the best, especially since she was the one who took the initiative.'

He continues his story with all the intensity his immaturity provides, demonstrating that he has no idea about a relationship between a man and a woman: "After a few months, I felt lonely; I knew that she was going out with someone else and that made me feel bad and brought back some memories. One day, when I was feeling melancholy, I called her and we met up. I surprised myself; without planning it I asked her to get back together. She was also surprised and told me that she had to think about it because she was going to give me a series of conditions. We continued seeing each other and my feelings lit up again. After a year, we got married. At first things went well, but afterwards routine kicked in. For

CONTINUED

---

10. This is what amateur psychology calls a trophy wife, a woman that one shows around to prove one's success with much younger, attractive women. This case has many elements of emotional immaturity; what we call elsewhere in the present book the socialization of male emotional immaturity.

me, it was exhausting to know that she expected me to dialogue, to spend time with her, and to talk. All those things sounded strange and foreign to me. After two years, everything had vanished, disappeared. The worst part is the image I was presenting to my siblings, cousins, friends, and professional acquaintances.

"I don't want to bore you any further, because history repeated itself when I was sixty-four; I fell in love again, this time with a divorced woman with three children, like myself, and lots of money. She was foreign; I met her on a holiday. We are now on the verge of separating; I decided to come to you because I read one of your books and thought that you might be able to help me repair this new relationship, although I am not even sure that I want to fix it."

This is a severe case of incapacity to love due to lack of knowledge of the basis of a stable emotional relationship. The diagnosis is clear: serious emotional immaturity. We must here reiterate an idea, which I have hinted throughout the book: in order to be happy with someone else we must be happy with ourselves. His lack of cultural and moral values, coupled with the absence of any spiritual side whosoever, are also quite astonishing. This patient is a child of the times, driven by hedonism on the one hand and relativism on the other.

5. Couples Can Undergo Crises

All married couples will experience crises, even in stable and positive relationships. They happen for no reason, other than the enormous complexity of living together. In other words, the script of a shared life in common demands some critical moments.

Because such crises are inevitable, we must remain alert for their eventual arrival. A marriage is like a ship about to start a new voyage over perilous seas.

Having a solid, well-built ship is only the first requirement in ensuring a safe journey. Neglect and carelessness can drive even an otherwise sound ship to ruin. For this reason, just as a sea captain must be trained to take care of his ship and conscientiously keep his logbook, so must married couples receive adequate training in love and pay constant attention to maintaining it.

In the chess board of our emotional lives, both feelings and intellect play important roles, in their intersection with culture and spirituality. Four key components—affection, intelligence, will, and spirituality—must be present if we are to win at the game of love.

Clinical case 5

Since we are discussing problems within the couple, there are illnesses affecting both people. Consequently, treatment is more complicated because the solution to the difficulties in question requires a double psychotherapy, the so-called couples therapy, which is a laborious, subtle, and lengthy process. Let us look at another case.

A fifty-one-year-old man, who is a successful engineer, has suffered from commitment-related panic syndrome since his thirties. He has allowed himself to be loved by

CONTINUED

Clinical case 5 CONTINUED

the women he has dated, but he has only been interested in going out and having a good time. When a woman demanded a formal relationship, he fled, disappeared, and experienced anxiety and psychological distress. This has been a constant all his life: "It's hard to admit it, but I never imagined getting married unless an exceptional person turned up, and even then I never thought I'd actually go so far. That was my idea. I have many friends, who separated one after the other, and they went through dramatic situations fraught with hard feelings. I've been greatly influenced by my parents, especially my mother, who was my teacher. She was a great reader and a big fan of classical music; she was also very clever handling my father, who was an authoritative man with a strong personality, quite proud of himself and arrogant due to his success in the legal profession. I am the youngest of four siblings.

"While I have always been very reasonable, I learned from my mother the importance of emotional life and how to manage and express it. I've seen such grave errors in my friends' marriages that I said to myself: 'Surely the same thing will happen to you.' My mother insisted that this was a very negative attitude and that I should keep my eyes open to the arrival of a woman who could satisfy me. I have also been influenced by a close sister, who is a psychologist.

"When I was forty-one, I met a thirty-five-year-old single woman at a dinner party. She was doing her postgraduate degree in art. From the beginning, I was captivated by her elegance, the way she talked, her posture, and, most especially, the

CONTINUED

Clinical case 5 CONTINUED

mixture of sweetness and professional drive she exuded. She was writing a doctoral thesis.

"I saw her that day and that was it. I liked her; however, I didn't ask for her phone number, maybe because I didn't want her to think I was interested. A month later, my friend, who had organized the dinner party, had tickets for the premiere of a play. He told me that she would be there also. I was delighted because I wanted very much to see her again. The four of us, including my friend and his wife, had a great time. After the play, we went to have a drink and we had the chance to talk a bit more; it was then that I realized that this woman could be important for me. I could not explain it, but I thought: 'This woman is worth it; she can maintain a conversation; she is pretty; she is uncommonly self-confident but feminine at the same time. . . .' I told my sister and she said: 'Call her and ask her out.' I didn't tell my mother, as I was waiting to see how events unfolded."

He then proceeds with an interesting remark:

"Some of my friends got married after their forties to women in their twenties, almost half their ages; in every case, it ended badly. For one reason or another, sooner or later, their marriages fell apart. They were all well-respected professionals with sound financial footings. Due to those fiascos, their problems multiplied—children, money, very ugly situations. All those thoughts started running around in my head, as I thought about having anything to do with that woman. My mind went back to the old refrain, 'Don't complicate your life, don't risk it, look at all the failures around you, wait a bit,' and things like that.

CONTINUED

"I started thinking about her constantly and wanted to call her, but at the same time I thought: 'If you call her, you'll see what happens,' and that possibility scared me. I was in that situation, when suddenly one day she called to invite me to a presentation of her future thesis. . . . I went; that day I realized, in my forty-first year, I had finally found the woman I'd been looking for without knowing it for many years. While she gave her presentation, I kept looking at her eyes, at the elegance of her hands, at her motion with the pointer towards the paintings, about which she made sharp, refined, and astute comments. . . . As she talked, I thought: 'This is your wife, you found her. . . .' I don't want to stretch the story for too long. We started going out and, in a few months, we got married. My parents were delighted and my sister gave her full approval.

"We got married after only a few months, but I discovered what love is in all its richness. Everything went fine until the fifth year of marriage, when we went through a difficult stage, because of my personality. I think this was due to two specific reasons: 1) my previous independence; and 2) my hypersensitivity—every remark from my wife, regardless of how mild it was, affected me greatly.

"We attended couples therapy and worked everything out, probably because of her good sense and because the behavioral patterns prescribed were very specific and correct. . . . The treatment lasted for three months and afterwards everything was fine again.

"Several months ago, we had another crisis, this time colored by differences of opinion about how to raise our

CONTINUED

Clinical case 5 CONTINUED

children, who are nine and five. We have different ideas about discipline: I am quite open-minded and tolerant, while she is rather strict and, in my opinion, too much so. We have often argued; on a few occasions, we have exchanged harsh words and gone for days without talking to each other."

And he continues thus: "I had heard about crises and problems with children, but it is difficult to accept that this is happening to oneself. I kept thinking that this is the sort of thing that only happens to someone else. We went back to the psychiatrist, who helped us understand the problem with great skill, guiding us in the best way possible.[11] I thought: 'I could never have imagined, considering how much in love I was when I got married and how much I love my wife, that these difficulties could arise.' I never thought about separating, but it hurt me a lot to see us arguing with one another and spending days distant from each other. I have learned to focus better on our problems, when they first appear, and to look for external help."

This is a notable case. Prudence is important, but it can be combined with a touch of audacity. One offers perspective, while the other the offers ability to take risks. Life is often an equation with contrary elements, which we must learn how to reconcile.

---

11. Such discrepancy is very common. The woman usually spends more time with the children, thus having a better grasp on their character, shortcomings, and points needing correction. The man, who spends less time at home, becomes more permissive and dismisses negative aspects of behavior. It is necessary for these positions to reach a compromise; each spouse must give up a little, guided by common sense. This sort of therapy, when well directed, normally has very positive results.

6. Two People United in Mature Love Retain Their Individuality

Two people become one, but nevertheless, they remain two. This is the beauty of love. The challenge is not to suppress others and change them to become what we want, but to respect their freedom and personality.[12]

Love is not just a feeling; mature love comprises decision, will, and intelligence, which are the other components in the equation of love.[13] In order to reach this state of dynamic balance, love must be skillfully and patiently carried out. This combination of two into one will never be static, fixed, or completed. Love is dynamic; it is constantly in motion.[14]

Clinical case 6

Let us now consider a couple where he is thirty-five and she is thirty-three. He owns a parking garage with several employees: "I have always had a strong personality and I am used

CONTINUED

---

12. The only exception would be when the character of the other spouse has a very negative feature, which gravely affects life and threatens the balance of the relationship. At any rate, I want to insist once again on the importance of dialogue and respect. Both members of a couple must have the intelligence and ability to give way in order to find common ground. This is one of the tasks of the psychiatrist and the psychologist: to become a mediator between the two, to facilitate the achievement of reasonable and positive solutions.

13. I direct the reader to chapter 6, in which I present a series of ingredients without which love cannot develop fully. Love is a complex feeling in which the emotional and the intellectual are equally important, and in which will serves as a mediator between them. I will insist on this complexity throughout the book, as it is one of the key ideas, which I want to impress on the reader's mind.

14. Love is thus perfectible and defectible. It can improve, if looked after, or deteriorate, if not.

Clinical case 6 CONTINUED

to giving orders, since I had to take over my uncle's business when he died; I was only twenty-seven."

"My parents divorced when I was twelve. It was a big shock for me. On top of that, I saw my father insult and physically abuse my mother. I try to behave as different as possible from my father, but I must admit that when one of my employees doesn't do things my way, it makes me angry. I think I have inherited many things from my father, but I have learned not to be as aggressive as he was."[15]

She is a homemaker, caring for the house and their children, who are nine, seven, and a few months old. Speaking about herself, "I have always been a shy, reserved person because I had a hard time with my family; I am the middle of five children and I always felt a lack of love and attention at home. When I met my husband, I noticed his jealousy; I thought it was very sweet that he loved me so much that he could not handle other boys looking at me or trying to talk to me, but I had to be careful with other men around, lest he think that I paid them more attention that I paid him."

The relationship went badly almost from the beginning. "I feel like I've lost my identity; I always do what he wants and on the occasions that I've tried to resist his dictatorship, his reaction has been so aggressive and so full of threats of

CONTINUED

---

15. As previously explained, there are two kinds of learning: imitation and contrast. The first copies positive features and healthy identity models. The second works the other way around: it consists of doing the opposite to what one has experienced. As expressed by this patient: "I have learned from my father how not to treat a woman and how not to be aggressive."

Clinical case 6 CONTINUED

separation, that I have ended up realizing that it's not worth the effort it takes to resist him. I am not happy with such an imposing man."

Both have come to therapy, but she is the one who is burned out, usually diagnosed as burnout syndrome,[16] after so many years of a poor relationship. "He has never agreed to look for help because he insists that we must solve our problems on our own and that I just have to accept the fact that he is the head of the family and let him run the household. . . . I feel pounded down; I have lost my motivation and he has such a strong, inflexible, and authoritarian temperament. . . . I think that if you can't help us, the best thing for me will be to leave and take my children with me and just focus on them. They have witnessed scenes in which their father has treated me with threats and all sorts of insults."

He attends therapy against his will, convinced by his wife's sister, who has providentially intervened to make him understand the need to seek psychological help. His

CONTINUED

---

16. This syndrome was initially named by Schwartz and Hill in 1953 in the context of a study of nurses working in psychiatric hospitals in London. It referred to low morale and chronic exhaustion. A more precise scientific description was given by Herbert Freudenberg in 1974. The symptoms are as follows: emotional exhaustion (physical and psychological fatigue), dehumanization in the execution of daily tasks (depersonalization, insensitivity, growing indifference), lack of personal satisfaction (including a negative opinion of one's role or, in the case we are dealing with now, a deterioration of the marital relationship that appears as a consequence of exhaustion), and some stress-related symptoms (tiredness appearing before any effort is undertaken, anxiety, nervousness, undefined bad feeling, sadness, apathy).

Clinical case 6 CONTINUED

interview is not easy, because he finds it difficult to understand that many of his reactions have caused their problems: "That's just how I am, and what I need my wife to do is to learn to accept me for me. She knows me. . . ." He is impulsive and disinclined to accept anyone's advice. Changing his behavior will not be easy.[17]

In psychotherapy, we have tried to teach him to soften his character, try not to impose his opinions so much, grant his wife a wider psychological space, be more affectionate with her by showing small gestures of thoughtfulness, apologize more often, and avoid showing affection only at night. The response has been slow, but it has eventually occurred.

In her case, we have tried to help her heal the wounds from their damaged relationship. His willingness to ask her forgiveness was a very positive step in the right direction.[18] Psychotherapy aims at substituting neurotic behaviors and negative attitudes with positive ones.

He tells us, in a moment in which improvement is obvious: "I've learned many things since our therapy began; for example, I thought that the other person had to accept your character, that you are who you are and that's that. You have convinced

CONTINUED

---

17. We have before us two completely opposite personalities. He is primitive, active, and impulsive; he acts without thinking and finds it difficult to stay silent. His impulsiveness provokes him to spring into action, mostly with words, without considering the consequences. She is secondary, passive, and reflexive; she delays her responses, tends to stay silent, and thinks about consequences before acting.

18. In couples therapy, this often yields excellent results; one of the spouses recognizes on a large scale, as if keeping a ledger, that he or she has made mistakes and wants to apologize. In this case, he has taken this step and the situation has taken a radical turn for the better.

Clinical case 6 CONTINUED

me that, if you try hard, you can correct those features of your personality hurting the other person. . . . I have failed greatly in this; nobody had told me so clearly how to improve my marriage; now I feel better and avoid acting impulsively, which is one of the things that made my wife suffer most."

7. True Love Gives More than Takes

This idea is relatively easy to understand in the initial stages of being in love. When we are discovering love, we wish to please the other person by offering the best possible image of ourselves. Later, as time goes by, this need gives way to routine. Then the seventh tip becomes important: true love means giving more than you take.

What does giving mean? Giving something is often understood as depriving ourselves of it. This belief is false. When I give something willingly, I can perceive my strength, my worth, and the control I exercise over my own person; I also realize that I am capable of giving someone else priority and of putting him or her before myself. The important thing is that I do it not as an obligation, but as a self-gift, which makes me a better person. I am filled with the best of intentions and, like a river, I overflow my shores and in doing so, flood the other person. Giving myself helps me to grow as a person.[19]

---

19. This was very well explained by the German thinker, Josef Pieper, in his book *About Love*, in which he says, "In every conceivable case love signifies much the same as approval. This is taken literally in the word's root: loving someone or something means finding him or it *probus*, the Latin word for 'good.' It is a way of turning to him or it and saying, 'It's good that you exist; it's good that you are in the world.'" The approval contained in this idea is more precisely an expression of our will. To love is to give and to feel inclined to be happy when the other person is well

To put it differently, more joy comes from giving than in taking or receiving. We have all experienced this sensation when trying to make someone around us happy. Why? In this generous action, I become aware of my vitality; I understand all I have inside; the desire to do something good for someone else emerges naturally. It is like a need to spend myself on the person I love, a careful process of giving oneself; I favor the other person, I welcome him or her, and I want his or her daily life to be as good as possible. It is a protective instinct applied to everyday life. This is a mood producing a very special feeling of inner well-being. In married love, the proximity is such that each is a witness to the other's life and experiences.

Selfishness is contrary to love. The selfish person is moved by egotism, aims to be the center of everything, and to receive more and more, because it is never enough. The outcome is these people end up coming face-to-face with their true self; the unveiling of their own resounding narcissism leaves them dissatisfied and unhappy.

What is love made of? Love is a reciprocal gift and a natural reality experienced by humans from the beginning of time, aimed at the fulfillment of the person. True love uplifts us and makes us more human. This reciprocal giving plays an important role in the definition.

---

and happy. Josef Pieper, *Über die Liebe* (1972), published in English as *About Love*, trans. Richard and Clara Wilson (Chicago: Franciscan Herald Press, 1974).

In *Love and Responsibility,* John Paul II talks about the difference between using a person and loving a person. In the former case, one treats a person as a means to an end, whereas in the latter, generosity, as expressed in the affirmation of the other person's worth, plays a fundamental role in the path, which starts with attraction, continues with good will, and ends in friendship and commitment: the happiness of the other person is our own happiness. Karol Wojtyla (Pope John Paul II), *Love and Responsibility*, trans. H. T. Willetts (San Francisco: Ignatius Press, 1993).

Clinical case 7

I do not refer now to a clinical case because the following case study concerns a couple, who managed to develop a relationship based on the principles grouped under the present "tip," serving as an inspiration for all of us.

The case involves a couple, sixty-four and sixty-two years old. They have six children between the ages of twenty-nine and eighteen. Both are civil servants—he, a lawyer and she, a doctor. They tell us their story.

He says, "We've been married for thirty-one years and before then we dated for a year and a half. I have always had a clear idea of marriage because of my family environment: my parents were very religious, but they never sent us to a religious school because we were seven siblings and only my father worked outside the home, managing an agricultural estate. My mother looked after the house. We went to a state-run school and all but two of us went to university. Our house was very small; because I was the second youngest, I always inherited my sibling's things, such as shoes, shirts, underwear, etc. At home, money was always tight. I remember hearing my mother talk about our money problems, always with a good sense of humor.

"The most important thing they gave was their example: hardworking, stable, joyful, and very committed to their respective tasks. When I started university, I had to combine my studies with a part-time job in a supermarket near home in order to help with the household expenses. My mother was a truly extraordinary person; I have seen her devote herself to my father and to each of us. She always took the worst— the most difficult tasks, the worst food, etc. She also had a

CONTINUED

Clinical case 7

profound religious sense, not prudish or exaggerated but truly sincere. I was looking for a similar woman and I found her at the guitar lessons, which I started attending during my third year of law school. I saw her, talked to her, and immediately realized that I was both physically and psychologically attracted to her. It was a while before we started going out due to her being very busy with her medical studies. She was also a member of a choir."

She says, "I would marry my husband all over again. He is a man I admire: hardworking, honest, and a good father. He is a bit of a scatterbrain; I try to help him be more organized. Our house is not very big. If everybody leaves their things all over the place, they can end up taking over the little space we do have. My husband was not very affectionate at first, but I've made him so little by little. I used to tell him, 'I want you to kiss me, to tell me nice things, and to look after me and the children when you are at home.' He is rather calm, sometimes too much so, and whenever we have a problem he always says, 'You'll see how we'll work things out.' I, on the other hand, am more nervous and worry about everything."

I ask her, "How have you managed to build such a positive relationship with your husband?" And she answers, "I knew what I wanted. I am an only child; that defines you because your parents have put so many of their hopes in you, keeping you from wanting to fail them. My father was a doctor and my mother a speech therapist. Both taught me what love really is—I saw it in them and in their selfless dedication to each other. When I got married, they gave me two

CONTINUED

pieces of advice: "Never go to sleep without apologizing to your husband, if you've made a mistake, or without sorting out anything happening between you during the day; better still, never argue."

"Living together took some managing: solving money problems, which in our case have been frequent; educating the children in our faith and giving them small household responsibilities while they were very young. Some make the beds, others prepare breakfast, and others shine shoes. I have two daughters, who are stars at ironing a shirt! All of them are involved in looking after the house in different ways. I am happy because I have a well-functioning family, a wonderful husband despite his little shortcomings, and children struggling hard to build a good life. My only regret is that two of my children didn't want to study. That was hard for me. I work at a hospital in the mornings and spend the afternoons at home, looking after the house and surrounded by my children."

I ask them both, "When you've had a disagreement, a big argument, or a typical 'bad day,' how have you worked it out?" She answers first: "At the beginning of our marriage, we had several big arguments as usual at the start; we had long, tense days without talking to each other, but afterwards we learned to dialogue, to apologize to one another, and to see things more moderately, with common sense. . . . We've always avoided trying to score points over each other, to win arguments at the other's expense. Additionally, we try to see everything with a certain sense of humor. I don't think we've had a big row for a long time. I love my husband. Sometimes, he does things that annoy me, but I can cope with that."

CONTINUED

Clinical case 7 CONTINUED

He answers: "My wife knows how to handle me, but I am a bit childish, although much less so than at the beginning of our marriage; sometimes I find it difficult to let go of something. She has taught me to get over my anger quickly and move on. My problem is that I am quite a scatterbrain and not very organized—traits annoying her a lot—but I'm trying to get better. We always try to work out our disagreements; from the beginning we agreed not to aim harsh words at each other.[20] The main thing is to look after the relationship, to make it positive, and to respect each other a lot. It is important to make life happy for one another; I must admit in that regard, she always wins."

May the reader draw his own conclusions. This last case study embraces a score of wonderful examples.

---

20. Many problems within marriage are the consequence of using harsh words with one another, words aimed at inflicting as much pain as possible. We must teach people to control themselves and speak with moderation and tact.

Part II

Maintaining
a Happy Marriage

CHAPTER 6

The Alchemy of Married Love: Seven Ingredients

What Keeps a Relationship Going

At this stage of our psychological path, we will examine the ingredients for a lasting love to be achieved. This path begins after we have left falling in love behind and arrived at married love. The first of these is short-lived. The second soon arrives; it is real love, worked and molded with various raw materials. We have to restore love as it deteriorates over time. We must repair it, transform it with our experiences, and polish it to make it better, while keeping in mind a foundation principle: in order to be happy with someone else, we must first be happy with ourselves. We must sand the rough edges of our own character, eliminating the obstacles to clear communication. This job must be undertaken gradually and progressively to attain a mature personality, the starting point in the lifelong task of integrating the seven ingredients of married love.

As we have seen, two people in love are able to offer themselves in full. That mutual offer must encompass several dimensions: physical, psychological, spiritual, and biographical. Reducing such a special encounter to a corporeal experience, while leaving the rest of the ingredients undeveloped, robs us of love's richness. Let us list these components: feeling, philosophical inclinations and shared beliefs, intelligence, will, compromise, and dynamic process. Combining these seven elements is what I call the engineering of married love. We shall explore each in detail.

The ingredients of love must be combined harmoniously. Before advancing any further, we should stress that our aim must be the combination of all love's components with balance.

I. Feeling

Love is much more than a mere feeling

In this sense, we must be precise to avoid the oversimplification of love. Love emerges from feeling. It appears when we find someone with whom we want to share our life. Falling in love is one of the strongest feelings that exists. It can be like a lightning strike, Cupid's arrow or the *coup de foudre*. It is a form of fascination. These are unforgettable, delightful, and intense moments. Other times, things take a slower pace, advancing step by step, as they should, toward the ultimate state of being in love. In this process, the last stage is reached when we say to the other person, "I don't understand life without you; you are an essential part of my life." It is admiration, absorption, desire to be with that other person, and exclusivity.[1]

Feelings are perfectible and destructible; they can develop for better or worse. Consequently, proximity and the passing of time

---

1. Lorenzo de Medici said that love is *appetite di bellezza*, the appetite for beauty. See *The Autobiography of Lorenzo de' Medici the Magnificent: A Commentary on My Sonnets,* trans. James Wyatt Cook, Medieval and Renaissance Texts and Studies 129 (Binghamton, N.Y.: The State University of New York at Binghamton, 1995), pp. 35–7. In everyday language we say, "You are mine, you are my life, I need you." This idea is key.

cause a wide array of emotional colors to emerge, making us go from the rose-colored initial stages to a large variety of colors, which reproduce life in all its complexity, including sadness and happiness, a full chromatic landscape where all emotions must be faced with maturity.

Love is a feeling and a decision. It is not limited to emotion; it also implies determination, which means deciding to cultivate affection and dedicating all the resources necessary to care for and protect it.

While love resides mainly in the emotional world, we must clarify what feelings are. Feelings are attitudes, positive or negative, which drive us toward or away from the object or person before us. They can be the cause of a strong attraction or an obvious rejection. Neutral feelings do not exist; neutrality has negative connotations. Let us think about boredom; at first sight it appears indifferent or undefined but is a closer cousin of melancholy and serves as the bridge to sadness and depression. Feelings control our behavior. Our lives can be focused either on love,[2] in all its varieties, or on hatred.[3]

This feature is important. Our decision toward love does not mean letting ourselves be directed by what the heart dictates. Rather, it means guiding ourselves with intelligence and will. In this sense, love is a long-term investment requiring short-term effort and strategy. How could we leave one of the most

---

2. Love shows many faces, although we are focusing on married love. Other aspects are: love for our job, which can degenerate into a disordered idolization of work; love for nature; love for truth; love for ideal concepts, such as freedom, democracy, fair play in sports, etc.

3. On other occasions, hatred guides behavior. Some subscribe to the popular saying, "an eye for an eye," and sacrifice their lives to revenge, seeking that moment when they will finally be able to strike their enemy in his or her weakest spot, but such behavior is unhealthy and can produce neurosis.

important elements in life to the whim of the violent winds, the ups and downs so typical of youth!

To say that love is a feeling, which comes and goes, not easy to control, is a false idea. Rather, feelings must be enlightened by intelligence, which illuminates and clarifies the circumstances. Will must also participate, pointing toward the target and helping to overcome obstacles. Both will and feelings promote stability. The biggest enemy of love is indifference, a lukewarm state in which feelings have been neglected, and lose strength.

From the most scientifically psychological point of view, love is an emotional state comprising a reciprocal exchange of reinforcing, positive, and gratifying conduct. They include the four facets already listed: physical, psychological, spiritual, and historical.

All love relationships experience difficult and disheartening moments. Even the best of loves, if not zealously tended, will diminish in quantity and quality.

The stages of love

Married love goes through several stages. The first stage is falling in love, which helps the two parties to know each other. Courtship precedes it, in which both show the best of themselves in order to satisfy expectations. Courtship has generally more to do with appearances than with reality; it is right that it should be so, but within certain limits. There are a series of strategies, which help us to charm our potential lover and foster the development of new love's three prerequisites: admiration, physical and psychological attraction, and the need to be with the other person as much as possible, exclusivity.

In this initial sequence, desire goes before being in love. At the beginning, it is a centripetal force coming from the outside in; it causes surprise, the initial fixation on the other, and the desire to learn the secrets of heart or mind of the other. A strong curiosity, like a magnet, attracts us to the second, centrifugal stage, which comes from inside out, caused by the need to seek the other. To be in love is to be enchanted, absorbed, spellbound—the prisoner of an irresistible drive towards the other.[4] To fall in love is to use all necessary resources to move the relationship forward: friendliness, beauty, hope, the need to be with the other, sexual attraction, and so on.

To love is to choose another person in order to focus on and put him or her at the core of our personal project. To choose is to select one among the multitude of people before us, to stop in front of that person, to call that person by his or her name, and to enjoy his or her beauty and personality. In these initial steps the face acquires a special role, because the whole body relies on the face.

The next stage corresponds with the initial phase of an already established love, in which emotions give more room to intelligence. It includes living together, which is one of the most difficult experiences in life and which demands constant learning. Both must learn how to handle the other in everyday life. Life within a marriage is the art of understanding and compromising, the latter meaning to think first about the other, especially when we are sure that we are right. Married love needs to be an equation between proximity and distance. If this is achieved, the strain of routine is more easily avoided.

We will now move from theory to reality, as we look at a clinical case study, useful for the illustration of these ideas.

We have a young couple. He is thirty-five, a lawyer and works with over two hundred people. She is thirty-five and works as a fashion designer. Both come from stable, middle-class families.

---

4. Within the plurality of its manifestations, we will now focus on this dimension of love: love is a force that pulls us; a tendency; in Latin, *vis apetitiva;* in French, *affection profonde.*

They have been married for six years, after they dated for two years while seeing little of each other due to his legal education abroad. After being married for a year and a half, he left her and moved into an apartment. She tells us, "My husband worked all day long, from Monday to Saturday; he had no time for anything else. We saw each other on Sundays; maybe we would go shopping together, but mainly he spent all day resting and there was no dialogue between the two of us; he was neglecting me. . . . Since I only worked in the mornings and had the afternoons free, I started taking language lessons. We went to a psychiatrist, who made my husband understand that his lifestyle was pointless and taught me some strategies to attract him."

Now a new conflict has arisen, compelling them to seek help again: "I have discovered that my husband began a relationship with a new secretary. I found out by reading his phone messages, but he had been behaving strangely for some time. He would come home late and often said he had to attend to dinner meetings. I found some restaurant bills, but I talked to his boss and he told me that there had been almost no such dinners. This evidence has made him confess at last. I am devastated. I still can't believe it."

He gives us the following account: "A new secretary joined our department more than a year ago. I was very impressed by how pretty and helpful she was. She was my personal secretary. I was physically attracted to her from the beginning, but nothing more. However, we had to spend a lot of time together and I sometimes told her about my life; she did the same. She is twenty-four and had just split up with her boyfriend. She was having a hard time. Sometimes we went for a drink in the evening, but nothing further. Things progressed gradually. She called me one Sunday because her car had been stolen and she needed my help; I went and spent all day with her . . . and my wife has probably told you the rest."

I ask him, "What do you feel for her [the secretary]?" And he answers, "I like her. I am attracted to her and I have fun with her. She never gives me trouble; she's always happy. It's been nice, but I have two small children and I don't want to break up my marriage. My wife is very badly affected and I want to start over. That woman has already left my department and the company. I know it will be difficult for me not to see this woman; I am used to being around her, but I owe my wife a lot and I think I've behaved like a teenager."

At the beginning of the therapy, she told us the following: "I forgive him and I am going to try and forget this, but I need time for my wounds to heal and for trust to reappear; I never imagined that my husband could be unfaithful."

We have designed a behavioral program with specific rules for each of them, although obviously he will be bearing most of the weight. We have suggested four steps for him:

1. To apologize to her and tell her that he wants to win her over in the same way as when they started seeing each other.

2. To tend the small details in everyday life: to make her life pleasant; to make sure there is more dialogue between them by looking for the appropriate moments; to call her once or twice a day; to run some errand for her; and so forth.

3. To finish work earlier, so he can spend more time with her and the children.

4. To share more activities—going out to the movies or to dinner, taking a trip, exercising together as they used to, and the like.

The patterns for her, initially, are:

1. To keep her forgiveness in mind, a very generous act, and to try to progressively forget the infidelity; that is her challenge.

2. To try not to bring up her husband's past mistakes in moments of tension.

3. To try to avoid arguments over little everyday things and to try not to use harsh words; to try hard not to be irritable; and to rid their conversation of verbal aggression or insults.

4. To progressively resume intimate relations.

In this case we have seen love's first two stages: falling in love and the initial stage of established love.

The third stage is that of mature love. It usually emerges around midlife, once the relationship already has a firm foundation and each has learned much about the other. No stage is free from problems in everyday life, especially because the epidemic of divorce scourging our society has a twofold immediate effect: first, divorce is strongly contagious in our over-informed society, where conduct receiving much attention tends to be imitated; second, this leads to the propagation of the idea that love is inherently fragile and aspiring to lasting love is very idealistic, even a fool's errand.[5]

This third stage, mature love, can come under attack from an environment, which presents breaking up as the solution for the smallest relationship difficulties, while trivializing divorce. It is important to remember the role played by intelligence, will, and common beliefs. We refer now to the last: spiritual married love transcends to a higher dimension and is nurtured by the

---

5. Today's media have surrendered to sensationalism; magazines and TV programs take a morbid interest in celebrities' marriages. They constantly bombard us with the latest celebrity divorcées, exhibiting their miseries in full detail. The only condition of interest seems to be that their lives are broken. These are disoriented times. Our defense must start with our education and intelligence.

supernatural. What do we mean when we say that married love has a spiritual dimension and what does it offer a relationship? Christian spirituality can fill marriage with love, strength, intensity, and scope; and everything has the possibility of becoming easier, if God is intentially involved. Let us not forget what the gospel says: *God is Love.* In other words, *God is Mercy.* When life is motivated by spirituality,[6] love has a new inspiration and a different flavor because giving becomes easier. This effect is visible even in unrequited or imperfect love. Christian faith gives married love a stability of structure, which facilitates giving ourselves generously after the model of Christ. In this way, love becomes natural and supernatural, physical and metaphysical, horizontal and vertical. In Seneca's words: *homo res sacra homini,* man is something sacred for man.[7]

Without a spiritual dimension, due either to neglect or denial of its necessity, there is an empty space that human love cannot fill; difficulties in everyday life will inevitably arise. Man is a dissatisfied and thirsty being by definition. Only a friendship with a personal God quenches such thirst. For married love to succeed without a transcendent dimension, natural love in which human virtues shine must be present.[8]

---

6. This means love is not superficial, but includes a deep and overreaching Christian sense, which arms the person with the best answers for a lasting love, inspired by the figure at the core of Christianity: Christ.

The essence of Christianity is not a life philosophy but much more: being Christian means first *knowing* Jesus, second, *loving* him, and finally, *identifying ourselves* with him.

7. Seneca, *De vita beata* (On the Happy Life).

8. Such virtues should be based on the cardinal virtues of prudence, justice, temperance, and courage. Human virtues are those natural qualities, innate to human beings. Humility, simplicity, generosity, and the disposition to serve others are usually counted as being among the most important. Some interesting works on this are: Josef Pieper's previously cited essays on the virtues; Peter T. Geach, *The Virtues* (Cambridge, UK: Cambridge University Press, 1977); and Peter Ackroyd, *The Life of Thomas More* (London: Vintage, 1999).

One of the best tools for caring for a relationship is having a common transcendent goal. It is telling the other person, "I want what you want"; this begins a common project in which each leaves his or her life in the hands of the other. As I said at the beginning of this book, love means saying, "I am not interested in a life that does not include you." Therefore, true love seeks commitment; I commit myself to you and I place my life alongside yours. If love is not true, and somewhat less profound, a sense of temporality will ensue until it falls apart or we get bored with each other. Christianity offers the possibility of marriage being elevated to the level of a *sacrament*. As a sacrament, marriage is a sacred experience, united to Christ, who teaches the couple the real meaning of love. Christ is the witness of the marriage union as well as the mediator throughout their marriage. When invited into this marriage covenant, he helps the couple overcome their conflicts and ensures that the relationship progresses and has a happy ending.

In the stage corresponding with mature love, we can start to talk about our real-life experience. We begin to share the accumulated knowledge that each of us treasures; we hold in common many specific lessons about life, its principles, and its rules. Maturity implies knowing ourselves as a prerequisite to knowing the other person.[9]

The art of life in common

Love involves both dependence and independence, freedom and imprisonment. Finding the right balance between distance and proximity is important; the difference between being together and having our own space is likewise important. As occurs with all types of balance, a certain amount of instability exists.

---

9. This knowledge helps us remember that nobody should be an absolute for the other person. Everyday life shows who we really are.

To love someone is to give and forget oneself, seeking happiness in the happiness of the other. Perseverance in this regard is heroic and a human miracle. The conditions needed for such a goal to be achieved are multiple: we must learn to yield in arguments when they do not involve fundamental issues; to promote a fruitful dialogue; to gratify the other with words and actions; to have a common project; to make life pleasant with those little details often going unnoticed; to give each one personal space; to learn strategies for interpersonal communication; to arrange a system of reciprocal rewards or reinforcements; to learn to surprise the other person with novel plans; and to learn to shelter and protect. Gaining such knowledge requires effort and a sporting sense of fair play. Those seeking life in common learn to face conflicts and difficult situations by employing two essential strategies: 1) moderation of judgments, trying to avoid excessive drama; and 2) learning to communicate under stress.[10]

Here, social intelligence interacts with emotional intelligence. It means knowing how to live with another person, avoiding conflict, looking after the other person, paying attention to their emotions, and developing positive everyday habits. This includes avoiding harsh words, derogatory comments, and insults when discussing personal issues. These principles must be kept in mind at all times.

The author John Gottman[11] has conducted extensive studies in this field. In his work, *What Predicts Divorce*, he writes:

---

10. I have insistently stressed that love is not merely a feeling but also an informed decision. Committed love is a transcendental resolution, with all its implications. Immature loves are nothing but provisional, non-transcendent relationships. See Juan Ramón García-Morato, *Creados por amor* (Madrid: Eunsa, 2008).

11. John Gottman, *What Predicts Divorce* (Mahwah, N.J.: Lawrence Erlbaum Associates, 2002). This same author draws a line between successful and unsuccessful marriages, stressing the importance not only of the depth of their love but also of their capacity to present themselves to one another with special dedication.

"I can predict if a couple will divorce after attentively listening to them for an hour." Along the same lines, Gottman points out that communication within the couple is one of the most difficult skills and must be given learning priority; one of the most important measures is to learn to give the other person the kind of love, which they strongly desire. It is a selective learning, a precise and patient training, all the details of which cannot be apprehended in a short while; it requires attention and dedication. As with all important things in life, it is achieved progressively; we must think of ourselves as apprentices to a skillful and knowledgeable craftsman.

For a healthy life in common, the best psychological resources must be employed. Possible ingredients are multiple; their selection depends on the needs and nature of the other person. Today it is normal for both members of a couple to work professionally; therefore, a good and clear distribution of domestic roles must be achieved, along with a kind of adaptational attitude to solve conflicts.

I will proceed with a psychological case, which should be of interest to the reader.

This couple had been married for fourteen years, knowing each other for two years. She is forty-one, and works in a gift shop, and says about herself, "I am quite easygoing and I love my job. I am a bit messy, impatient, and neither very punctual nor very good at time management. I didn't learn those skills in my parents' house. I am a very enthusiastic person and love challenges; we have three children, aged twelve, six, and three."

He is forty-two, works in a chemical firm, and says about himself, "I am rather shy, private, very organized, and excellent at time management. I don't tolerate poor work performance; I love reading and classical music; and I adore my children, whom I want to raise with strict discipline, just as I was when I was their age."

Their most frequent friction points are her lack of punctuality and organization, coupled with his rigidity and resistance to change. Tense situations are common. He explains, "What bothers me most is her lack of punctuality; she is always late. Her disorganization at home and lack of planning also bother me. A few days ago, we had a dinner party at a friend's house. We were asked to be there by 6:15 pm; there were five couples invited. Around five, I told her that 'I wanted to leave at six and that I don't like being late. When I asked her to start getting ready,' she said yes, but I noticed that she carried on doing things around the house. At 5:30, I told her again, but she was on the phone for quite a while. Before six, I asked her to hang up and get ready. She started getting ready after 6:30; I went to the living room and picked up a book and decided not to say anything else, but I was very nervous. She's done this many times; it's a classic. At seven, when she was finally ready, she told me that the problem had been her sister's phone call; she'd had something important to tell her. I told her that I was fed up and that it was always the same. We started having an argument, in which she started insulting my parents and shouting very harsh words. I told her that she was very unprofessional and that her fellow workers told me that she was always late and didn't carry out her duties properly. The argument escalated and woke our oldest son, who heard all the things we said to each other. By then, it was 7:30. I called my friend; I told him that we couldn't go because I wasn't feeling very well. They insisted that we go, even if for a short while, but we weren't fit to go anywhere. I was in bad shape; she was angry too and itching to dig up my past mistakes. I began sleeping in a different room. The following week, we came to see you."

Our team gave her the following goals:

1. To learn the other day's lesson for once and for all: almost every time I go out with my husband, I start getting ready at the time we should be leaving the house. I will take punctuality seriously. It has become a bad habit for me, and I need to correct it. This detail greatly affects my husband. I must train myself to meet this specific goal.
2. To try to remember that while having an argument I tend to tell my husband very hateful things about his family; I will try to break this habit because some of the things I say are difficult to forget.

Our team gave him the following goals:

1. To try not to tell my wife the same thing again and again. She says that the more I repeat myself, the less inclined she is to do what I ask. I must remember what the psychiatrist says: a psychological law states that excessive repetition of a given idea wears out the recipient, causing an opposite effect to that intended.
2. To try to avoid arguments after situations similar to the one I have related; I must leave the room to gain self-control.

In most cases problems in married couples arise from different points of view, especially at the beginning. If they mount up, they can develop into a bigger problem, which causes exhaustion and leads to the creation of a list of complaints.[12]

---

12. The list of past grievances must be locked away in a cupboard. In couples that do not function, this collection is always trying to get out, causing further problems. Controlling it helps during a conflictive situation.

2. Sexuality

To love is to feel attraction

The second feature of love is a tendency or inclination to share everything with the chosen person. It is the desire to be together and to choose the other person above all others. In classic literature, such desire is called *prima inmutatio appetitus*—a motion or appetite that can only be satisfied with proximity. This is the natural inclination in love: to reciprocally seek each other. As we have already said, this inclination has four facets: physical, psychological, cultural, and spiritual. Each of them has its own sphere, but all share a common trait: an inclination toward the other person. In this section I will refer to the importance of sexuality, and in others I will tackle the psychological and cultural facets.

Sexuality is one of the key languages of committed love. Others include verbal and nonverbal communication, the creation of a common project, mutual help in all of life's predicaments, and bodily intimacy.

Sexuality is total communication in which the body has the starring role. Sexuality must be harmoniously integrated into the couple's common project. It has its own space and role in this common program. It cannot be the foremost priority because it would otherwise become an obsession; it must have its own proper place, and every couple must learn it.

Pleasure is a powerful engine for married life. Intimate relations operate within a system of reciprocities in which pleasure is the consequence of well-oiled preliminaries: communication, psychological understanding, compatibility, mutual help, and the joy of being comfortable with the other. Sexuality is a natural drive—it is on the human "hard drive"—and the important thing is to be able to give it its right space and let it play its right role.[13]

Two important factors to note: Sexually, man is more basic, primitive and impulsive, which means that he is more elemental and more easily excited; a mere stimulus will trigger all physiological instincts. This can cause the sexual act to be carried out too hastily and end prematurely, not allowing the woman to participate fully and causing her an acute sense of frustration. If these circumstances recur with some frequency, the woman can end up losing interest in sexual relationships. Woman requires more elaboration; she is secondary and reflexive. This means that her stimulation is slower and more demanding; she requires certain positive and pleasant psychological conditions, which are generally unnecessary for men and not missed when absent.

Tenderness is vitally important and love's oil. It involves delicate and soft actions; words and motions must acquire fine nuances. The three main means of communication must fill up with emotion: verbal, nonverbal, and subliminal. Seduction is an art lying between the neat and the diffuse, the mysterious and the ethereal. With the passing of time, monotony causes sexual relationships to lose their initial passion, especially if the emotional aspects, are not looked after. A man, who smiles while reading this and thinks it of little interest, probably knows very little about how to treat a woman.

Sexuality within a couple must be about much more than sex. It must be a way to communicate, to share, and to collaborate. We must try to achieve an intelligent sexuality in which all these elements are present. We must try to give our sexuality our own style, because with the passing of time new modes and styles will

---

13. We must distinguish between sex, which is a physical act, with its own anatomical and physiological triggers, and sexuality, which involves a much richer reality: psychological, spiritual, and biographical.

be discovered. The important thing is not to let routine take over by always repeating the same patterns.[14] The best way to achieve a positive sexual relationship is the combination of art, talent, and cooperation. We must learn the keys to prepare the other person for the culmination of orgasm. The orgasm must not be made into an icon; rather we should try to achieve a full relationship in which the physical, the psychological, and the historical combine in a beautiful melody. Love is the complete realization of human potential; all these elements must participate in it, combined according to the personality of each one of us.

Sexuality is important for a couple

Sexuality in married life must be vindicated. It is something magical and wonderful. As with everything that is good, it must be treated appropriately and respectfully rather than carelessly. We must have clear ideas. For this reason, the ideal is that each party possesses a good emotional education. Sexuality defines a couple. Very often, conflicts arise as a consequence of a bad sexual relationship, ending in tension, disagreements, and arguments. We must try to find the right moment; women must understand that men are more active and require a more intense sexuality, and men must understand that women require more preparation and tenderness.

The way a couple conceptualizes sexuality will impregnate all manifestations of their relationship. It is essential to solidly

---

14. Often, if not renovated, sexuality within the couple becomes a soulless, tiresome, and cold routine. In other words, always having sexual intercourse during the weekend, at the same time, and following the same pattern ends up becoming insubstantial and boring.

Many couples consult me after falling into an apathetic and uncommitted sexuality; I always recommend a change in their sexual habits, both in frequency and quality.

integrate sexuality into the couple's common project, because it is present in all dimensions of life; it permeates all psychological corners and, if well placed, will keep the couple securely united. Sexuality is something very precious and must be seen with affection and respect; it is part of the commitment of a couple, leading to parenthood. Our psychological and clinical experience will also be of use in this instance. Let's consider the following case.

We have a young couple. They have been married for two years after seeing each other for another two before that. He is thirty-two. He studied economics and works for a trading firm. He defines himself thus: "I like sports; I go to the gym at least for one hour a day and I play soccer. I am organized, persevering, and thorough; I think that I use my head more than my heart, but within limits." After meeting him in a few sessions of psychotherapy, we must add that he is obsessed with order. For example, he allows no one to touch even a book or a piece of paper in his office. He is excessively rational, narcissistic; he checks his weight daily, does physical exercise at home while going to the gym every day, and is also egocentric. His wife says, "He seldom thinks about me or about what I'd like." At thirty-three, she is remarkably attractive and is also very outgoing and personable. She studied public relations and works for a company, which organizes events for a publishing firm producing newspapers and magazines. She defines herself as follows:

"I think that I am good at public relations, very close to my friends, and open. I love life and try to help those around me to enjoy it too. Now, I am not happy with my husband and I want to separate; I am obsessed with that idea because he's disappointed me enormously. He either works all day long or spends all the time in the gym or playing soccer with his friends. I feel neither loved nor valued. I want him to look after me, to love me, and embrace me; he says that he loves me and that, materially, I have all that I could wish to be happy. We argue because I get angry when I see how selfish he is." She proceeds, "Before I married I thought that sexuality was a wonderful thing, a total commitment to the other person, and you can imagine my surprise that even in that he's proven disappointing. I am a religious person and, until now, I never thought of separating, but I am now beginning to see that he's incapable of changing."

Let's see what he says. "She already knew how I was and how important order is for me; I don't know what she is complaining about. Sports have always been an important thing for me; before we got married, she came with me a few times to watch me play soccer with my friends. I didn't know that marriage was so difficult and that women needed so much attention. It's too much for me. . . . Besides, I have always been quite argumentative, but now we argue all day over small things that have spiraled out of control and I don't know what to do. The situation is bad. I never thought it could get this far; the worst thing is that we've said terrible things to one another."

Therapy is not easy, especially because she is burned out, and she flatly refuses all suggestions to alter her attitude toward her husband. On the other hand, she insists that living together right now is all but impossible; she wants him to stay with his parents, insisting:

"I need to think about all that's happened. I need time; right now, I am in no shape to make any important decisions. I don't know whether to separate for a time, or once and for all, or, as his mother has suggested, consult an expert in Canon Law to obtain an annulment. I don't know what to do, but I do know that I don't want to be with him under the same roof, because everyday life is extraordinarily difficult for me."

After a couple of months, she feels better. They have seen one another every week; both are undergoing a transformation, especially him, who is the one really needing to change his ideas about life in common and marriage. She has made several demands in writing: "I want him to correct the way he treats me, which involves taking away some things and adding others. At the same time, I've explained to him that he needs to work on how we communicate with each other. So far, he's made me feel very empty in this regard."

Time will tell, regarding whether this couple can overcome their severe problems. He is becoming aware of his psychological shortcomings and practical and theoretical limitations. She is feeling more receptive.

We are our body and our body represents us

One of the most important manifestations of married life is the intimate interaction, which is achieved through our body and our inner life. While we are our body and control our body, we are much more than our body. Sexuality affects multiple strata of our life in common; for this reason, we must stress the importance of a functional sex life. Sexuality grows when accompanied with deep understanding and tenderness, when at its heart exists a private dialogue, and when attention is paid to the details of the encounter. Sexuality is something precious, making men and women more human. Sexuality is like a smile. Behind it, there is much more than a facial expression; it is supported by many sensations at once: happiness, hospitality, self-affirmation and support, friendship, and other positive feelings. The sexual act implies two people's giving themselves to one another totally, because each wants the best for the other person. The sexual act is true love, if backed by a common project, a commitment. Otherwise, it can easily develop into the utilization of the other, becoming exploitation.

In young couples, frequency and intensity take center stage; in those that have been married for a long time such frequency decreases, but sex should not therefore be less important. As I have already said, sexuality within marriage is a great symphony, rich in small nuances. We must look for the right moment, in which sex acquires a special intensity, such as holidays, trips, or when the haste of everyday life is put aside.

Let us look at another case concerning sexual difficulties:

This case involves a couple married for sixteen years: he is forty-five and she is forty-one. He tells us, "Sex has seldom worked for us, because my wife is rarely in the mood. She is always too tired, too busy, too worried about our children, having four, from ages three to fourteen, or having her period. She also claims that I am always thinking about the same thing; she's gone as far as telling me that I am obsessed with sex, which hurt a lot. In my opinion, she hasn't had a proper sexual education. She's had nobody to talk to about this, other than a couple of close friends and yourself, Dr. Rojas. She is an affectionate person, but always stops herself because she says that otherwise we'll end up having sex. Lately, I've tried to talk to her, but I think that your role could be essential. You are a doctor and this is the first time that she has consented to talk about this to anybody."

His story makes it clear that, from his point of view, the topic has been wrongly focused. The moment has arrived to change this pattern.

She says, "Things are not as simple as my husband makes them seem. He doesn't realize how much work I've got at home and how many jobs I have to carry out. On the other hand, for me it's more important that he talks to me and embraces me than having sexual relations. My husband is always in the mood, but I need calmness. I've already told him this, but not too often because I didn't know how to put it. I love him and know that he is a hardworking man. We are religious people and want to sort this out."

I have always said that if a couple seeks psychological or psychiatric help, it is a good sign, because it means that they want to find a solution to their problems. This is so, with the case in hand. We designed a program of individual behavior and reciprocal reinforcements, aimed at helping her see that changing her attitude and approaching sexuality from a different perspective can improve her marriage.

3. Common Beliefs

Having similar spiritual foundations

Sharing a faith that permeates everyday life, but is capable of transcending it, is another basic pillar for a stable and lasting emotional relationship. Without a spiritual dimension, the human dimension is imperiled and the future of a couple is much more fragile. A transcendent dimension fills life with motivation and reasons to live and hope. By excluding God, we strip life of solid arguments and reference points. We deprive ourselves of that which upgrades love and fills it with the noblest of ideas. Without this help, there is no reason not to change partners when something does not work out. This way of thinking is based on hedonism and permissiveness. The fruits of this type of relationship are consumerism and relativism.

These errors—hedonism, consumerism, permissiveness, and relativism—lead to human beings with no references. People easily become lost and are subject to a fluctuating and unstable emotional life with severe personal and family consequences.

The report entitled, *When Marriage Disappears*, shows that in the United States there is a clear difference between stable and unstable couples: the former normally involve people with university degrees, while the latter are common among people with a middle educational level.[15] The report offers the following idea: although marriage remains a valued institution, it has become a luxury item for the more poorly educated classes. In other words, the broken home rate has risen in the US among those with a medium educational level, while decreasing among those with university degrees.[16] At the beginning of the 1980s, only 2 percent of children whose mothers had a university degree were born outside marriage, compared to 13 percent in cases of medium education, and 33 percent in cases of basic education. This has changed, and by the end of 2010, the percentage was 6 in cases of university degrees, compared to 44 percent in cases of medium education, and 54 percent in cases of basic education. The celebrated "American Dream" seems to be slipping away. Three cultural changes can be detected: first, a more permissive attitude about the definition of marriage and love-relationships; second, stronger probability of changing partners throughout life and a higher incidence of infidelity; and third, a tendency of less-educated Americans to marry less, live together outside of marriage more, and break off their relationships with greater frequency.

---

15. The study indicates that marriage as an institution is losing credibility among the American middle and lower-middle classes. In other words, divorce and parenthood outside marriage have increased among people without university degrees. See W. Bradford Wilcox and Elizabeth Marquardt, *When Marriage Disappears: The Retreat from Marriage in Middle America* (Charlottesville, Va.: The National Marriage Project, University of Virginia, 2010).

16. It is obvious that a marriage with solid human values, even if without a spiritual dimension, will be stronger, and enjoy sturdier foundations. Recent research has complemented the classic works cited in the text.

There are a number of works on the same topic, but I will mention only some because the literature is so extensive. Terman and Oden (1974) observed a positive relationship between happiness within marriage and religious commitment. Burke and Weir (1976), in a statistical approach, observed that higher education has an enormous influence on the happiness of married couples. Some years later, Freudinger (1983) demonstrated that religion was a key factor in matrimonial stability for American women. Filsinger and Wilson (1984), for their part, observed that religiosity was the most relevant variable for marital stability. Another interesting work, published by Johnson et al. (1988), focused on 313 Mormon couples, stressing the following ideas: first, that actively religious couples divorced very rarely and, second, that the least happy marriages were those in which the women worked at home, looking after the house rather than having a job outside the home.

Clark and Crompton (2003) highlighted how in parts of Canada couples with a religious education showed long-term positive growth and increased chances for stability.[17] Paloutzian and Park, in their famous *Handbook of the Psychology of Religion and Spirituality,* insist on the same idea with very revealing data.[18] The contribution of Patrick Fagan, working for the Heritage Foundation, is also worth noting; he states that religion plays a decisive role in the consolidation of solid couples

---

17. *https://www150.statcan.gc.ca/n1/pub/11-008-x/2006001/9198-eng.htm.* Stephanie Coontz's work, also published in Canada, is equally interesting. It analyzes the close relationship between a good religious education, Catholic in this case, and a stable marriage. See Stephanie Coontz, *Marriage: A History* (Toronto: Penguin, 2005).

18. Raymond F. Paloutzian and Crystal L. Park, *Handbook of the Psychology of Religion and Spirituality* (New York: Guilford, 2005).

and the significant reduction of divorce rates.[19] Equally, Ahmadi et al. (2008) have proven that individual religiosity has a direct impact on marital satisfaction; by using questionnaires for the objective measurement of results, they found a direct correlation between religion and a satisfactory marriage.[20]

In another interesting work, Brown, Orbuch, and Bauermeister conducted a lateral analysis on the effect of religiosity on black and white urban couples in the US, concluding that the effect of religion on marriage stability is very significant; black women insisted on the importance of attending religious services and actively participating in them; for white women, this was almost twice as important.[21] Similarly, Lehrer attained comparable results regarding not only the stability of married couples, but also the positive effect of religion on economic and demographic factors, showing that religiously active couples have more children.[22] In Germany, Kraft and Neimann

---

19. Patrick Fagan, *Why Religion Matters Even More: The Impact of Religious Practice on Social Stability*, Heritage Foundation, December 18, 2006, *https://www.heritage.org/civil-society/report/why-religion-matters-even-more-the-impact-religious-practice-social-stability*.

20. For this study, the Enrich marital satisfaction scale was used; this scale establishes a series of very specific items with which to evaluate the relationship, including, for example, verbal communication, sexual relationship, plans in common, and criteria for raising children. Khodabakhsh Ahmadi, Esfandiar Azad marzabadi Azadmarzabadi, and Seyed Mahdi Nabipoor Ashrafi, "The Influence of Religiosity on Marital Satisfaction," *Journal of Social Sciences* 4, no. 2, February 2008.

21. Edna Brown, Terri L. Orbuch, and Jose A. Bauermeister, "Religiosity and Marital Stability Among Black American and White American Couples," *Family Relations* 57, no. 2, April 2008, pp.186–197.

22. Evelyn L. Lehrer, "Religion as a Determinant of Economic and Demographic Behavior in the United States," *Population and Development Review* 30, no. 4, December 2004, pp. 707–726; "Religion as a Determinant of Marital Fertility," *Journal of Population Economics* 9, no. 2, June 1996, pp. 173–196.

(2009), working for the German Socio-Economic Panel, reached similar conclusions.[23]

Finally, the psychologist Annette Mahoney (2010), from the University of Houston, examined the role played by religion—its advantages and disadvantages—in matrimonial relationships and in parent-child relationships over a ten-year study (1999–2009) involving a large population sample. She concluded that religiously active families were more stable and less susceptible to conflict and domestic violence; infidelity, teenage pregnancy, and problems at school were also less frequent.

This section summarizes what numerous scientific studies have demonstrated many times over; namely, having common beliefs and trying to live them to the full in everyday life is beneficial for married life and the education of children.[24]

Thus, a religious dimension has proven to be decisive to a lasting marriage. If this appears to be self-evident from the outside, from the inside, as shown by statistical analysis, it is even clearer.

The Christian perspective

The three great monotheistic religions are, by order of appearance, Judaism, Christianity, and Islam. They are chronologically

23. Kornelius Kraft and Stefanie Neimann, "Impact of Educational and Religious Homogamy on Marital Stability," IZA discussion paper no. 4491, October 2009. This coincides with Gary Becker's theory on the predictability of marital stability and its relationship with a high level of education and religious commitment.

24. In another work, Wilcox, director of the National Marriage Project of the University of Virginia, and others proved statistically that the variable "religion" favors matrimonial stability. Using data from the National Survey of Religion and Family Life (NSRFL) for a sample of 2400 black and Latino individuals between eighteen and fifty-nine, they found that religion, race, ethnicity, and social integration were of paramount importance in this regard. Christopher G. Ellison, Amy M. Burdette, and W. Bradford Wilcox, "The Couple That Prays Together: Race and Ethnicity, Religion, and Relationship Quality among Working-Age Adults," *Journal of Marriage and Family* 72, August 2010, pp. 963–975.

successive. It was the first two that took the qualitative leap; the search for God was not started by men, but by God himself.

When experienced coherently, Christianity is a beautiful experience. It is not so much an ideological program as the knowledge of, faith in, and love for, a person. Married love benefits greatly from this perspective, if it is influenced by Christianity's decisive message of repentance from sin, love, forgiveness, support, and generosity.[25] Christianity can help develop love to the full. It has the potential to elevate love to the supernatural state. It teaches the logic of love as being generosity and service. These gifts can help make the family a stronger institution, a sanctuary sheltering human life in all its stages.

We must defend religious freedom, which is sacred not only privately but also publicly. Current times have seen the growth of two negative trends: secularity, which tends to hide religion and marginalize it to the private sphere; and fundamentalism, which does the opposite by trying to impose it on others by force. The right position is admitting that God has asked humanity to follow the path of true love, which involves the person as a rational and spiritual whole, wherein an environment of freedom is essential. When religious liberty is effectively recognized, our individual dignity is respected, allowing us to search in a sincere manner for goodness and truth.

True human growth benefiting society and its institutions is easier for Christian families. Family is the basic social unit and marriage should be its foundation. As Richard John Neuhaus said, "No state, no party, no academic institution, no other community of faith has proposed such a comprehensive and compelling vision of the family in the modern world. . . . The

---

25. In true love, we cause the other to show his or her best, develop his or her full potential.

Church's teaching is a bold proposal that can inform public thought and action."[26]

At the same time, traditional married love and family values are currently under growing attack by neopaganism and hedonism. A culture failing to accept the transcendent is one where the person is seen as an object rather than as a human being. Our task is to demonstrate human truth: what man is, what it means to be human, and what love is. If we lose our perspective, we will find that we are open to manipulation by those around us. We will also discover that our moral codes become shaky and unclear. Such a loss of perspective makes a caricature of freedom.

4. Will

Love is a feeling and a decision

There are two types of theories on love. One is full of clichés, repeated again and again, that lead to the use, abuse, falsification, and manipulation of the word love. This is the liquid or romantic love so popular nowadays. The other is solid love, which involves a much more substantial notion; loving someone is offering him or her the best that we can offer, wanting all the best things for that person. Between these two types, there exists a wide range of loves, oscillating between the *liquid and yielding* and the *solid and firm.*

Let us clarify the nature of different ideas of love:

- *Diligere* is love with will. We can call it effective love. It is a love in which determination is important. It is a mature love, where will plays a key role.

- *Amare* is love focused on feelings. We can call it emotional love. Everything about it revolves around emotions.

---

26. Richard John Neuhaus, "To Propose the Truth: The Catholic Moment Requires Five Transformations," *Crisis*, April 1, 1994.

- *Caritas* is love with generosity. It is based on the idea of gift, and offering. It includes a multitude of good virtues.

Married love should be articulated through this threefold manifestation of love. The Classical tradition also contemplated other dimensions of love: concupiscent or erotic love, benevolent love or indulgence, and complacent love or friendship. We may also add maternal love and fatherly and brotherly love.

Love is a gradual feeling; it is made of several stages that progressively evolve: approbation, desire, a tendency toward possession, and an inner feeling of happiness and energy. I have said it before and I want to insist on the following idea: love is not limited to a feeling, because it also involves a decision and the determination to work toward it.

Feelings act like mediators between basic instincts[27] and reason. They are prompted by emotions and the other six components analyzed in the present book. They have a significant sexual dimension, are affected by beliefs, must be supported by will and intelligence, require a commitment, and must be understood in their dynamism.[28]

The role of will

Will is the ability to advance toward what is good for us; it is a sign of psychological maturity. Love needs will to overcome

---

27. Animals have *instincts,* human beings *tendencies.* The former are innate and triggered by external stimuli. Once set in motion, they cannot be restrained. They satisfy a strong need, such as hunger, thirst, or sexual appetite. The latter are acquired; they can be controlled by human beings, by cutting the stimulus reaction chain through the operation of intelligence, emotion, will, and spirituality. These four variables are essential for the governance of our conduct.

28. Life has so many surprises around every corner; reacting only to the latest event is a grave mistake and can have nefarious consequences. Will and intelligence are essential, if we aspire to a mature, stable, balanced, harmonious, and lasting love.

conflicts and to correct failings in our life in common. This is neither the case with the "being in love" stage nor with the initial moments of a relationship. During this early phase, our perception is taken over by overwhelming emotions and wonderful experiences prompting the desire to be together. The lover tries to develop the best self he or she can offer in order to avoid disappointing the other person. It is at a later stage that will starts to play its role.[29] Why is will necessary? What is its role? Will operates daily to improve love, to prevent it from deteriorating with time, and to remove all obstacles to our life in common.

Will is a feature of intelligence. We must remember that will tends to incline toward what it perceives to be good; however, this can be a false good. Thus it is important to train our will to seek the true good.[30] Will does not operate apart from reason, but rather in cooperation with it. In order to improve my marriage. I try hard to correct my mistakes and defects, the small or not so small things that I do wrong to the other person. I decide to act; I am conscious of the way I treat the other person, so we can approach our disagreements differently and contribute to a better life in common. This is the role of will. Will is essential for marital life.[31]

---

29. It has appeared only at the very beginning, when we have decided whether the other person is worth our attention, whether we share the same values, what in him or her is true and what is mere appearance, and whether that other person is what we are looking for.

30. A strong will is one of the clearest indicators of personal maturity.

31. Nowadays, many erroneous notions are being taught as natural. Among other things, we say that love cannot be commanded and that it is subject to all the vicissitudes of life, impossible to control. This common idea has had serious consequences, leaving love badly exposed to whims and frivolous attitudes.

I insist that having a well-balanced will and intelligence contribute to turning our love into a true, responsible, and lasting experience. These are confused times.

Will operates in a double dimension. First, we must want to achieve marital stability. This implies the determination to work for that relationship with actions and not only with words; we must also make the selection of the means with which we will carry out our decision, which requires a previous deliberation and the consideration of advantages and disadvantages.

Will involves wanting and selecting. It answers questions like, "How can I make my relationship healthier? How can I make it overcome all difficulties, all problems that will inevitably arise . . . because that is life." Will prompts us to take some specific steps for the attainment of our goal of having a solid relationship, capable of resisting difficulties, while being innovative.[32] This is what psychiatrists call motivation, which is nothing but advancing toward a target, propelled by our will. Things do not happen of their own volition but must be made to happen. Motivation reinforces will.

In short, we must put will and intelligence in charge of our emotional life. Both are superior features; their absence may have very severe consequences.

With will, all your dreams can come true

Love must be looked after day by day. Otherwise it becomes a routine; it loses strength. If not taken care of, the best of feelings can vanish or be taken over by apathy.

This fourth component of the alchemy of love will help in assembling two personal realities and psychologies. Without will, married life can degenerate into an association of selfishness, where each tries to satisfy their own desires without

---

32. Introducing new things and surprises in our married life is an intelligent action, which helps to renovate the relationship. One of the worst things for love is routine, when everything is known and everything has been discussed. Psychotherapy often works in this direction.

reference to the other; their lives become parallel, always separate and never touching. The final result is a precarious balance constantly threatened by conflict.

When love forgets, ignores, or minimizes the role of will, it becomes fragile, and sooner or later it suffers. It is like that love so frequently appearing in modern songs; turning its back on will, such love turns frivolous, superficial, light, and susceptible to being carried away by the next seductive stimulus.[33] Will improves with use. The governance of our actions depends to a large extent on how we manage our will. There are degrees of willpower. The summit is only reached after numerous small victories, small in appearance, while being essential to smooth the edges of life.

This fourth ingredient is not particularly popular, but it is essential. It is not fashionable and nobody talks about it, but it is nevertheless basic. When love is merely based on feelings, it is likely to go wrong, because will is an intelligent and practical response to the wear and tear of life in common.[34] Will is closely related to freedom; it must be fully integrated with love.[35] Its

---

33. If love is left unprotected, if it is open to other possible stimuli, it will eventually become volatile, and other people will change its course. Fidelity is made of natural instinct and prudence; it involves the practical intelligence of avoiding getting ourselves into emotional adventures, which can threaten our love.

34. An immature conception of love does not take will into consideration. This is typical of teenagers and young people in general and is the cause of unstable loves. We should not depend on our moods, but on our will. Independence from our inner fluctuations will provide us with an enormous freedom of action.

35. I want to mention a few relevant books regarding this issue of will. Paul Chauchard, *L'éducation de la volonté* (Mulhous, Paris: Salvador Éditions, 1973); Paul Jagot, *La volonté* (Paris, 1977); Robert Tocquet, *Les pouvoirs de la volonté*. Paris: Godefroy, 1986); Wayne Dyer, *Real Magic Areas* (New York: Harper Collins, 1992); Rafael Alvira, *Reivindicación de la voluntad* (Pamplona: Eunsa, 1988); Fernando Corominas, *Cómo educar la voluntad* (Madrid: Ediciones Palabra, 1993); Tomás Melendo, *Ocho lecciones sobre el amor humano* (Barcelona: Rialp, 2002). These references offer a wide range of perspectives on the issue.

role is to shape love and make it devoid of sharp edges, so that it is amenable to change. Will is one of love's less popular dimensions, but it is also among the most decisive. The triumph of will makes feelings solid and thoughtful without causing them to lose energy or vitality.

Love is based on a threefold foundation, constructed of intelligence, will, and commitment. There are more elements, as we shall see, but these three are of extraordinary importance. The will's task is to correct, modify, rehabilitate, and perfect love. Love requires a promise of our commitment to make this love last the difficulties, which will inevitably arise. In promising, we express our commitment to the continuation of this love.

The following case should help further explain the role of will in love:

This couple has been married for seven years after seeing each other for one and a half. They are forty-one and thirty-three years old and have three children. For the past year, they have been going through an evident crisis. She complains thus: "My husband works all day long. He leaves home at eight in the morning and doesn't come back until nine in the evening; he never has lunch at home, because he'd waste an hour and a half in commuting. He is always tired, overwhelmed, and often in a bad mood. With this economic current crisis, the situation in his company has deteriorated; they have laid off a number of people, and the environment is tense. With me, he has turned cold and distant; he is developing an authoritarian edge, which he didn't have before. When he wants me to run an errand for him, he asks forcefully, in a rush, and without saying thank you; he just commands me to do it. . . . We've had lots of arguments in the last few months, especially because his mother interferes and he hasn't been able to cut the umbilical cord with her. . . . I think that he rings her more than he rings me. Besides, when he talks to her, his tone becomes softer than with me. I have stood up to it and used harsh words with him: 'You are selfish, vain and only think about yourself. It is impossible to contradict you. . . .' I have told him that I am feeling less and less in love[36] and that he is falling off the pedestal on which I put him."

We see that the situation is truly difficult. She has left her job at a modern art gallery; she used to arrange sales and organize catalogs for new exhibitions. Her husband says, "Leaving her job has affected her badly; on the one hand, she feels frustrated; on the other, whenever I ask her to do something for me, she always complains or refuses. . . . She's been complaining for over a year that I don't pay attention to her, that I don't listen, and that we don't talk—and she's partly right—but she's always calling me names and, unlike everybody else, she doesn't value me. Then, there is the issue of my mother; they never got along and my mother is a bit edgy with her, because they have had arguments lately . . . To tell you the truth, I am a bit overwhelmed by the whole situation and that's why we are here, to try to find a positive solution. As I say, I always find a solution for problems at work, but here I am completely blocked."

Both show symptoms of burnout syndrome, which is a chronic fatigue leading to severe wear. He is more moderate, while she seems more aggressive and resentful. As we always do in these cases, we suggest three requests for each, in order to have an unbiased document to work with, while carrying out separate explorations with tests and psychological questionnaires to complete the personal profiles. The questions are:

---

36. Her remark is most unfortunate. By being too direct or insulting, all that we are doing is putting the relationship at risk, even if such remarks are the consequence of rage; these things are not easy to forget; they stay hidden, ready to leap out at a bad moment with hugely negative results.

1. What are the main areas of conflict, in order of importance?
2. What would you take away from, or add to, your spouse's character to improve your relationship?
3. The same thing, but applied to yourself: what would you take away from or add to your own personality to improve your relationship?

Both have provided us with this information, and we have contrasted it with their psychological profile, drawn up during their individual interviews.[37] In both cases, we emphasize the importance of exercising more will and intelligence. Both want to find middle ground; he is more resigned; she is more aggressive.

Here is the program for her behavior:

- I must try not to use strong words with my husband.
- I must not mention divorce.
- I must not talk about "being less and less in love;" this sort of language has far-reaching repercussions; it is not easy to forget.
- I must list three specific things, which he must do to improve our everyday life, always constructively.
- I must not use harsh words or an insulting tone to refer to his mother.
- I must create the conditions for a dialogue, free from verbal aggression.
- I must argue as little as possible and only about important issues.
- We must share positive things throughout the week.

---

37. It is always better to run the interviews separately, because that way the participants feel freer to express their point of view without being scrutinized by the other.

- I must run errands or do my husband favors without complaining.
- I must be careful with nonverbal language, grimaces, disapproving expressions, etc.
- I would strongly benefit from finding a job, even if the pay was low at first.

Here is the program for his behavior:

- I must try to get back from work earlier and spend more time with her and the children.
- When I get home, I must try not to go on about how tired I am or about the difficulties in the office or the company.
- I must always remember that my wife is the most important person, ahead of my mother, and I must prove it with actions.
- I must avoid spending all my time by myself, and thus ignoring my wife and children.
- I must call my wife a couple of times a day, to see how she is.
- I must be more affectionate, both in words and actions.
- I must learn to apologize when necessary.
- I must accept it when she disagrees with me, without making a big deal of it.
- I must surprise her every now and then with a plan to break up the week's monotony.
- I must tell her that I love her and that I need her.

After the first few sessions the relationship shows improvement. Both have realized the importance of will, by practicing that old saying, "Where there is a will, there is a way." Both have assumed that the heart and the mind must be fully committed. The sessions have been less and less frequent and, nowadays, their relationship is healthy. They have learned to use small strategies to solve small everyday conflicts. They have been very disciplined about reading several practical books on how to improve marriage.

5. Intelligence

Heart, mind, and culture

These three words are synonyms of feelings, reason, and education. Intelligence, the fifth component of the alchemy of love, incorporates doctrine and sense into the relationship without reducing passion or deactivating the magnet that drawing people together. This ingredient can also be unpopular, but such unpopularity is the result of impoverished vision and an old-fashioned approach to romanticism. Love between a man and a woman must be simultaneously emotional and intelligent. This is the way to achieve the necessary balance. Intelligence is the ability to synthesize. We must also learn to distinguish the optional from the necessary; we must learn to capture reality in all its complexity. Thanks to intelligence, we choose the best for each of us, the most appropriate. I have mentioned it already when talking about falling in love: making the right choice is decisive and for this reason all our senses must be engaged in it, even if such a decision normally presents itself when are young and we are overcome by passion. For these reasons, the intervention of intelligence sometimes seems difficult.

In these cases, lovers are characterized by youth and excessive passion. It is important, however, not to forget that intelligence is our best aid when confronted with a decision; it will help us to make the most appropriate choice for our own character. We must not let ourselves be blinded by external appearances. More importance should be given to inner human qualities, values, and a coherent lifestyle. The second task of intelligence is to facilitate ongoing learning aimed at improving our love: taking away what is bad and adding what is needed. A grumpy, disorganized husband, who doesn't cooperate with the housework, can be transformed with perseverance and intelligence into an affectionate, more organized person helping at home every day. In humans, learning is more important than instinct. In already established couples, learning is everything. Through our freedom, we set goals and objectives for ourselves, thus becoming masters of our own change through our ability to improve. This means the following:

1. Love improves through knowledge, both about ourselves and about the other person. By avoiding unnecessary arguments, we cut short possible situations of emotional tension, which in the long run wear the relationship out. This is practical intelligence. Ignorance kills love.

2. In humans, the substitution of instincts for tendencies interrupts the cause-effect relationship. Love can be managed with a well-balanced mind and with the knowledge that all problems have a solution; it is just necessary to find it. On the other hand, we must begin improving our relationship by improving ourselves. It is not easy to change others; we can only change ourselves, and only in a realistic way. If our relationship isn't working, we must detect where the problem is and take all necessary measures to correct it. We should not focus on conflicts but instead prepare to practice functional solutions. Just as athletes are always trying to improve their performance, married couples should show a similar impetus for improvement.

3. Forgiveness is of enormous importance. It is an intelligent action, full of meaning. It is recommended in all

circumstances. Long-lasting, well-balanced couples know that forgiveness is a basic ingredient in their relationship. To forgive involves both words and actions. The former are immediate; the latter take time. Forgiveness belongs to the realms of will and intelligence, but its roots are spiritual. Forgiveness and revenge are opposites; revenge hurts over time because it never forgets injuries and it is never satisfied. Forgiveness is very beneficial to our mental health, along with being a wonderful instrument for the improvement of our love.

A change in perspective brings a change in feelings

Intelligence is incredibly powerful; if used appropriately, it can be very beneficial. Love between a man and a woman must be an intelligent act because it gives love strong roots and the ability to last despite the usual difficulties. As with will, this may not be very fashionable, but it is not a question of turning love into a calculated and soulless equation. It is not that. Feelings must be kept alive and burning, but intelligence must be added in order to increase their strength.

I will try to explain it using the example of Beethoven. It is well known that this genius of classical music composed his splendid symphonies very laboriously, with constant corrections. He changed a movement, retouched a *ritornello,* polished the *finale,* and added new instrumental variations. His works of art were not spontaneous; they did not spring from his hands in a couple of weeks, but they suffered endless corrections until the result was fully satisfactory. A job well done will last. All work requires constant effort, guided by logic. Love is a work of art, the task of combining two symphonies into one.

Intelligence points out what needs to be improved and what needs to be done to ensure a harmonious relationship; this information changes our perspective on love. This trait is of enormous interest from a practical point of view, because it gives us the clue as to how to treat the other person. It is important to deepen our knowledge of ourselves and the loved one, as well as of the secrets of a harmonious relationship. By increasing such knowledge, we learn the way to live with another person.[38]

When love is nothing but a feeling without will or intelligence, it is constantly in danger, threatened by change and by ups and downs. Love can be neither too emotional, nor too rational. We must find the right balance, harmony, and moderation, in order to be able to analyze facts with common sense. Love needs passion, as much as it needs patience. It is essential not to keep a precise account of mistakes, failings, negative comments, or unfortunate anecdotes, because such minutiae kill spontaneity and generate tension and anxiety.

Having a successful professional life while failing in our love makes no sense, but it is something that happens very often. The talent for other areas of our lives must also make a mark on our love life by adding clarity, knowledge, and the ability to sweeten the other person's life and erase our own mistakes. All these come as a result of a well-oriented intelligence.

6. Commitment

Big things almost always have simple foundations

Loving is committing. Love is a great thing because of commitment. Committing to something means making a contract and

---

38. We progressively translate the hieroglyph of living with another person and sharing everything. Life in common must not be left to the mercy of the winds of chance or of momentary whims. If so, our relationship will inevitably sink. Will and intelligence are the two most solid arguments for improvement; he is a happy man, who can recall them when necessary.

taking responsibility for meeting its conditions. Loving is caring for, looking after, promising, and guaranteeing. Loving is choosing, selecting our companion for the future, and thus building with him or her a common project. Loving also involves stepping into the other's shoes and giving that person what we think he or she needs. Empathy is another key for a solid, ever-growing, and better love.[39]

True love requires the freedom of the loved one. This much is clear. Today, this might be difficult to understand, for love reveals a conflict of freedom. Personal freedom is compromised by love. This is why the issue is so important. Loving is committing in full, giving everything but also expecting everything; it is a reciprocal gift. We must make an effort to say yes not only now, but also in the future.

True commitment is responsibility and faithfulness. It is the road to happiness, which is the consequence of our actions. Faithfulness is an imperative of love, which must be achieved daily with small and specific actions aimed at protecting our love. Faithfulness is not a free commodity. Committing is placing ourselves at the service of love; such service involves toil, a dedication to craftsmanship, and to detail. Faithfulness is exclusivity. Faithfulness is loyalty, gratitude, and emotional stability in the present and for the future. Almost all great things rest on

---

39. When empathy is lacking, discord arises. This word is composed of *dis* (different) and *cordial* (heart or feeling); it thus means feeling differently. It will bring our relationship into a situation of intermittent conflict; the relationship will be commanded by animosity and unproductive daily struggles. If problems are not solved and no solution is found, communication will deteriorate; arguments in which both parties bring up past wrongdoings and insult each other will multiply and a dangerous environment will prevail.

The opposite feeling is concord, which is an agreement of wills; both parties yield and try to find friendly common ground. This is a positive symptom of love.

simple foundations. Faithfulness is the will to preserve and protect our love, to make it last, and to resist betrayal, neglect, and sporadic or lasting affairs. Faithfulness involves the will to toil against tiredness, conflicts, and routine.

In a relationship, faithfulness and stability usually go hand in hand, positively affecting all members of the family. Couples with a successful relationship take seriously the promises they made each other before getting married. They understand that the sin of adultery is destructive for all members of the family.

Commitment opens the way to having children. Children deeply enrich married love. How often we hear these kinds of statements coming from parents:

"Our children have changed our lives; they have filled us with hope, they are wonderful. . . . Now I remember that at first I was surprised at myself, spending hours in front of my son, playing with him and discovering every inch of his face, his smile, his hands, and his feet." A father told me after the birth of his first child, "I never thought that I could experience the sort of change that I underwent when I became a father; it is difficult to explain; you feel a new person and you discover what having a totally defenseless creature depending on you for everything is." Looking at your child, together with the spouse whom you love, is a wonderful experience.

Raising and educating our children is teaching them values. We must not forget that we are their first teachers; our example will be their reference.[40] When a couple has children, they transition from being merely friends and lovers to becoming

---

40. We educate more through action than through words. Educating is introducing love and knowledge into reality. Educating is opening our children's eyes to life in all its complexity and thus orienting them. The four main ingredients of education are will, emotion, intelligence, and spirituality. They are all closely linked to one another.

caregivers and teachers. For this latter role, we need structure, reference points, and clear aims.

Faithfulness is promoted by trust in the other person. Trust is belief in the other; faithfulness is will. There is gratitude[41] and true friendship. It is setting more store in what is good than in what is bad, not forgetting the goodness received from the other person. Faithfulness is what remains of faith, when faith weakens.

Love has a daily accountability

In the previous pages, I have insisted on an idea that I think is essential: love must be looked after with small details. The fabric of life is knit from a daily accountability in which lovers find ways to give themselves reciprocally. Love is the greatest task of human beings; there is no bigger feat or responsibility more important. Faithfulness is a joyful commitment made of generosity and renunciation. Faithfulness consists of constant and small acts of loyalty, which reinforce love. Life is long and many things can happen. Modern life offers us endless chances to abandon all our commitments; hedonism is all around.[42] Without faithfulness, selfishness prevails. All will look after their own needs before considering those of others. This selfishness is one of the main illnesses of love; one of its key symptoms is that we live our own life independently of the other. The man may take refuge in his job and do nothing but work. The woman, if she has children, may spend all her time with them and grow distant from her husband. Their lives take parallel routes, which rarely interact with one another. This is a sour and devastating

---

41. Gratitude is the heart's memory.

42. Even in these neopagan times, aspiring to remain faithful to the person to whom we have committed is still valuable. Faithfulness is an eternal value that cannot go out of fashion; it will always be a noble aspiration.

experience; it involves an emotional void and, at the same time, an "over-fullness" of ourselves. In such cases, urgent therapy is recommended to prevent the final sclerosis.

Today, there are plenty of choices for splitting up: separation, divorce, changing couples—all causing a lack of interest in keeping relationships alive, in giving the best of ourselves to try to save them from disaster. Rather, many couples choose the easiest course of action.[43] This epidemic is having terrible consequences—a multitude of broken couples that could have been saved if both members had accessed the necessary means to achieve a solution and had practiced a bit of patience. But we live in the era of the immediate: everything has to be sorted out right now. As we say in colloquial language, things are taken too lightly; when we realize our mistakes, it is normally too late.

According to this view of love, love is nothing but a momentary feeling, lasting for as long as it is able. The very moment difficulties appear, people begin to consider abandoning the relationship. We deprive love of the opportunity of achieving a solution; at the same time, we develop a defensive mechanism typical of our times: minimizing the importance of the rupture—"It's no big deal"; "That's just how things are"; and so forth.[44] Under

---

43. Nowadays, we want solutions to appear immediately. Conflicts in married life, however, need time and work, gradual changes, and constant corrections. We must learn to forgive one another, to start with a renewed energy. All this requires time. The immediate solution is to break up and look for someone else. The best solutions—working things out, assembling the pieces in their right position, gradually renewing love's objectives—require time.

Sooner or later, love will demand a psychological revision to adapt to new circumstances.

44. Two reactions are typical in these situations: first, the inability to work hard for a relationship going through a bad spell, and second, the trivialization of rupture.

Both are exponents [manifestations?] of a diminished society: frivolous, sporadic, changing, where feelings are interpreted lightly and informally. I have said it throughout the book: society has accepted emotional immaturity and lack of spirituality.

these principles, love no longer includes the promise of "forever." Eternity disappears and everything becomes temporary and relative; everything depends on the circumstances.

This results in a diminished love—"love lite"—without will, intelligence, commitment, or perseverance, subject to life's fluctuations and whims. Our permissive society indulges in this sort of love; love has become a commodity in a society marketing everything. It is like an exchange of emotional products, which I have elsewhere called mercurial love. Today's relationships are the same: they meet, change, seek, break . . . always on the lookout for the next experience.[45] Commitment is one of the features of true love. It makes love true and strong. It gives us maturity, self-knowledge, and the ability to give ourselves in full.[46]

7. Fluidity and Dynamism

Love is not static but dynamic

We now take the seventh step in our trip toward the alchemy of lasting love. The reader must not forget that this sequence follows a meaningful order. On the other hand, we must also remember that all these components need to interact within a structure, a mosaic, and a systematic whole; sound love requires an emotional scaffolding.

---

45. One of the clearest symptoms of emotional immaturity is fear of commitment, so common nowadays with people in their early thirties. They fear losing their liberty. It is yet another feature of that individualism so strongly pervading Western society.

46. Another symptom of immaturity is the instrumentalization of the other, or in other words, using others to achieve personal ends. The other is not chosen as a whole, but only for one reason: sex and the desire to maintain an uncommitted and shallow relationship for social reasons, such as the wish to be noticed, and so on).

Emotions go through three stages:

1. *Being-for-life,* which includes survival instincts and impulses.
2. *Being-for-oneself,* which is when we gain possession of our own self.
3. *Being-for-another,* which in turn includes two stages: the ability to be with another person and the ultimate ability to be one with another, to share and live a common life.

There is an objective dimension of love, consisting of a personal relationship based on friendship, communication, and shared experiences. That love is a dynamic process does not mean that the intimate relationship changes, oscillates, transforms, or is shaken as a consequence of the events and circumstances of everyday life. It needs to maintain some of the fundamental elements from which it was born, but experience dictates that life in common will be affected by many ups and downs for which we must be prepared. We must use our will and our intelligence to ensure that all these problems are solved in the best possible way.

We all know many couples, who got married on the basis of physical beauty, personal admiration, social position, economy, or a shared spirituality. But these circumstances can change abruptly, and we must be ready to handle what comes. One of the key symptoms of emotional maturity is the ability to adapt our emotional life to current circumstances without losing depth, beauty, and commitment. True love is capable of filling the heart. It is not only fulfilling, but also opens the way to a true surrender through its attractive and demanding path.[47]

---

47. We must vindicate love's strength, its importance in life, and its toil. Love is an adventure that demands the best we can give to the other person. And that is always hard; it demands that we commit to it in depth. I encourage the reader

Love as dedication and renunciation

Married love, the basis of the family, can only be preserved and perfected through dedication and renunciation. These two words gain prominence, as time goes by. We must pay attention to the other person and consider him or her our main priority.[48] Dedication is an effort, an act of will, a determination that must have a foremost position in our thoughts at all times; it must be granted its rightful place. The concept of renunciation is sometimes given negative connotations; it should be understood as saying no to ourselves in order to serve the other's interests.

Understanding that love is a dynamic process implies the operation of maieutics. This is the art of giving birth to an inner truth, the presence of which we have ignored. We must understand that married love hides an enormous wealth needing to be recognized and worked on. We must be able to extract each and every one of love's components. This may seem idealistic, but I do not think it is; it is an ideal, or wish; which will become a reality if we aspire to perfection.[49] Ideal love does not surrender to the mediocrity of the environment, but seeks excellence in the mundane. Married love is

---

to refer to Ricardo Yepes Stork's work, *Fundamentos de antropología* (Pamplona: Eunsa, 1996), which explains that ideals are an excellence of the human condition. I also recommend C. S. Lewis, *The Four Loves* (San Francisco: Harper One, 2017), where we can taste an analysis of human love based on commitment. From the early stages of psychiatry, in the early twentieth century, we recommend Victor von Gebsattel's, *Prolegomena einer Medizinischen Anthropologie* (Berlin: Springer, 1954), which combines a double vision: the study of the person and the point of view of a famous Central European psychiatrist.

48. This is a very specific objective. Our partner should be given absolute priority. It is the most important and most valuable thing; in my hierarchy of values, my spouse has the foremost place.

49. Aspiring to perfection is a noble thing, as long as we don't fall into excessive perfectionism, which is a form of sickness.

based on small positive details, delicate attention, frequent gratitude, and knowing how to yield. It thrives with expressions like "I love you," "I need you," "You are my life," "I want to give you the best I have," and "Forgive me."[50] This dynamism feeds on a wide range of actions and subtleties.

50. Spending many hours with our spouse is not the important thing here, because we must give priority to qualitative dedication instead of to quantitative dedication; whatever time we spend together must be rich.

CHAPTER 7.

Learning to Love by Loving: Some Interesting Cases

The Ability to Love Shows a Healthy Civilization

Throughout the book, we have been trying to establish concepts and describe the main elements for a lasting love, capable of overcoming difficulties and bettering itself. At the beginning of the twenty-first century, society has attained spectacular scientific achievements but has been incapable of transmitting the essence of true love.

Technology has brought us great progress. People are permanently connected and social relationships have reached new dimensions; they are, however, superficial, because it is impossible to have as many friends as we collect on the internet through social media. We have many options, but relationships themselves are often unsatisfactory. The ability to love should be the true indicator of a healthy, modern, and civilized society. We should ask ourselves, even if it sounds naive, whether young people in the West can truly love. Have they learned to do so? Because we should keep in mind that learning to love is the first response, which life requests from a young person. However, it is not easy to find a love that lasting. Everything is trivial. True love emerges from the encounter of two personal projects illuminating each other. An emerging love is a feeling with degrees of passion or emotion on an increasing scale, depending on its intensity.

An excessive drive toward superficial emotions is the cause of impersonal, anonymous sex. This also has to do with the growing idea of wanting everything and wanting it now. If love appears in these circumstances, it rarely has a good ending, because the process has been inverted; the house has been built from the roof down. These difficulties mean that many young couples, blinded by sex, cannot grasp a wider and richer perspective on love.

The Pillars of Love for a Couple

The pillars of married love are old and new at the same time; they are old as life and new because each era demands different things. When we fall in love with someone and choose him or her for our project, we place our bets on the values that person represents. I have already mentioned how important our selection is for the future stability of our relationship. Intelligent selection weighs the pros and cons; it assesses whether a given person is beneficial for us. Men want to be valued; women want to be understood. Human beings give priority to love over liberty; for this reason, they aspire to true love.

Married love is a satisfying sensation, a tendency toward the other; it is an act which must have a physical dimension, shared beliefs, will, intelligence, commitment, and dynamism. The seven ingredients are closely related. We must not deface love by reducing it to only one component. As stated before, love is more than just and a feeling; it is a decision an act of will, aspiring to mutual understanding.

I wish now to discuss meaning of loyalty and faithfulness. The former refers to true, legal, authentic, honorable actions. The latter is more specific and refers to the promises we have made to another person. Loyalty is being honest; commitment is being reliable. A loyal person is incapable of falsehood or of lying with words or actions, because of their personal values, namely, staying loyal to their principles. Faithfulness, on the other hand, applies to behavior based on trust and made up of love and duty; married faithfulness is a prime example. In short, we are loyal to our project and faithful to our spouse.

Love is the Soul of the Family

Married love is the origin of the family. Its three essential elements are love, economy, and education, which comprise the emotional, the effective, and the intellectual. All three must be present in the family, if harmony is to be achieved. Each one of them expands to show a wide range of possibilities.

Our family does not love us for what we have, but rather for who we are. This is the first emotional environment for the person and the natural habitat for true love and brotherhood.[1] We must also not forget the role played by the economy, which compels us to live realistically. Sobriety must be an ingredient; this requires not creating unnecessary needs and living according to our means. He who has more is not richer. A small degree of happiness can be achieved by being content with what we have and with what we are, while always trying to nobly ascend

---

1. The concept of brotherhood derives from having siblings, and from sharing things within the family. Families deciding to have no children, or just to have one, will have to face the problem of not having the means to teach generosity, the ability to yield, or to share.

Families with several children become a university in which teachers and students build a two-way road. In well-oiled families, as the son and the daughter end up following the actions of the father and mother; this encourages a fruitful rotation of roles.

in all material, psychological, and spiritual senses. Education comes later, in which we teach the best that we know. Educating is teaching other human beings what life is.

The family makes society more human. If a family is properly structured and psychologically healthy, it will be a school of good practices; the members of the family will face the world with energy and their projects will be full of strength, with willpower to overcome difficulties.

Some Interesting Cases

My experience as a teacher shows that case studies are very illustrative and often teach the clearest lessons. Classic clinical sessions in medical schools involve a patient, who has previously given informed consent, allowing a group of students to attend his or her clinical interview, in which the teacher directs and the students participate. I remember that when I was a student, such sessions were extraordinarily useful for me. I learned lessons through them that I have never forgotten. Let us then look at some instructive cases.

A typical story of emotional immaturity

The case involves a young couple. She is twenty-eight and he is twenty-nine. They have been married a year and a half, after seeing each other for five months. She didn't want to go to a university; she said, "it was too much work for me and I preferred working as a secretary; my father, who's very well connected, found the job for me." Her husband works in public relations in a hotel during the week and at the hotel's nightclub at weekends. In his own words, "my job involves having good contacts with the hotel's clients and organizing events, weddings, meetings, that sort of thing. . . . I think that I have a talent for human relationships."

She says, "We met at a party; from the beginning, he impressed me because of his good disposition and his way with people, as well as his physical appearance. We were introduced by a mutual friend and talked twice, but it was mostly small talk among other people there. A couple of weeks later we coincided again in the same place. . . . I went there with the intention of seeing him, and I did. I liked him a lot. After dinner, we continued talking and went to have a drink until the early hours. I had just left a very dramatic relationship of three years. My ex-boyfriend had left me and my self-esteem was very low; he had used harsh words with me and had insulted me for not having a degree, my character, and other things.

"I admit that I don't know how to be single. I've gotten used to always being with someone; that's just how I am. Every time I have finished a relationship, I have started another almost right away. I fall in love very easily. With this man, everything went too fast. Something strange happened, my two best friends had just gotten married, and I asked myself, 'When is it going to be your turn?' I started obsessing first over not having a boyfriend and later over marriage. I found him attractive, physically and psychologically . . . although he had a reputation both as a womanizer and as frivolous, since he was coming and going all the time."

He says, "I was a bit scared of marriage because I didn't want to lose my independence; besides, I know some people around my own age who are already separated, and they've had some truly traumatic experiences. What I like is to have fun, and my job is exactly like that. When we met, I had fun talking to her and comparing her with other girls, without thinking of taking it any further. It surprised me that she started insisting on coming after me. As time went on, I couldn't say no. Next, I met her mother and sisters and had lunch with her family a few times; almost without noticing, I got dragged into a relationship from which it was not easy to escape. I enjoyed being with her, we had fun, but from there to marriage is a long shot. Besides, as I have said, I was scared of marriage; for example, my sister, who's two years younger, is already getting a divorce. As I say, it was like a downward spiral, and, before I realized it, she was already talking about a wedding."

They had been seeing each other for a very short time. She summarizes these months as follows: "During this time, we went out constantly, saw other people, and had almost no time to talk about 'us.' I wanted to get married and thought that he fulfilled my expectations. I didn't know that marriage was so demanding and that living together could be so hard, because going with him to dinners and parties is very different from everyday life. I am a believer, but I have stopped practicing, partially because of the lifestyle I've led."

He says, "the times we were going out were good fun,[2] Even frantic; we met many people and finally got married. I didn't want to get married, to be entirely honest, because I lived very well as a bachelor; everything just happened too fast. Now, I regret it and realize that I was not ready; my mother told me so. I studied at a religious school, but I have grown cold in that sense in the last few years. I have had several girlfriends, but they never lasted long because I honestly didn't plan to get married until much later. Our marriage was set up to fail. After getting married, I had an affair with a girl, who turned up at the hotel. I worked long hours and soon realized the burden I had given

---

2. This is a very unfortunate way to describe such an important stage in a relationship. Going out together at the beginning is a key phase in which the two persons should explore each other in depth, show what they have to offer, and ponder whether what they are starting is worth pursuing. Do they have compatible personalities, similar points of view on life, similar socio-cultural levels, common beliefs, similar professional objectives, and so forth? An expression like "was good fun" sounds too shallow.

myself. . . . Soon, the arguments with my wife started, and we went days without talking to each other. Well, the usual in these cases. I am very bored with her."

She proceeds along similar lines: "I wanted to get married, settle down, and have a man who loved me . . . but everything has gone wrong. I thought love was wonderful and that having someone who loved you was the best thing in the world. It's been so disappointing. His cheating devastated me, although we were already in bad shape before that; we were very cold to each other. I didn't know him well enough, to be honest, and I had forged an image of him that didn't match reality. I let his facade as a public relations specialist hide how hollow he was inside."

We have here two cases of severe emotional immaturity, which is all too common these days. Neither was ready for marriage. Her emotional education was poor, they didn't have a common project with more or less solid beliefs, and they were not aware of the scope of the step they were about to take. Love may be blind when it arrives, but it will certainly see all when it leaves.

A difficult case with a happy ending

This case involves a couple married for sixteen years. They have four children, who are fourteen, eleven, eight, and four years old. A successful professional, he studied economics and works in international investments. His wife says, "He lives for his work—there is almost nothing else for him. I never thought that anyone could be so passionate about his profession, while neglecting his wife and children so much."

She comes to our office on her own, without her husband, and explains, "I have decided to separate because I can't stand it any longer. I almost don't see my husband; he is always attending meetings and working. He doesn't see his children, and I feel emotionally empty. I was very much in love when we got married, but I have been feeling more and more hollow. I have talked with a lawyer; things cannot continue like this. I chose the wrong husband. While we dated, I idealized him. He was quiet, serious, very formal, maybe a shade too introverted . . . but I thought he'd change with time. Nowadays, I would describe him as a cold human being, objective, critical about reality, and centered on his own personal goals. I was inexperienced in love; he was my first and almost only boyfriend. I only had a short fling with a boy, my age, during the summer months. It was a beautiful experience and marked me deeply, but the memory faded with time. I was cheerful, open, very talkative, and very social, and; the differences between us surprised me. I was intrigued by this reserved man, who barely paid me any attention, when I had having been a lot of luck with guys my age."

She continues, "He is a good person, but he only pays attention to his own interests. I am constantly expecting a loving word, some gesture, something . . . but nothing happens. We also have a sexual problem, which for me is serious; he seldom desires me. When he does, it is the only time he shows tenderness towards me, which infuriates me. It's beyond me. I've already told him on several occasions, but with no results."

Given the situation, I tell her that it would be helpful for him to visit me to see if there is a chance of fixing things before she takes such a drastic step. She tells him and he comes soon afterwards. He says, "My wife surprised me the other day; she told me that she wanted to separate and had talked with a psychiatrist and a lawyer about starting the paperwork. What has happened for her to want to take such drastic measures? She knew how I was before we got married. I am quiet, shy, not a very big fan of social life, very hardworking, responsible, serious, organized, and not fun.

My wife complains that I talk little and don't express my feelings. I tell her that I've always been that way and she needs to adapt to it. I cannot believe that she wants to separate. I say, 'You have got everything you could want with me.'"

I tell him that he is not affectionate with his wife, that he has no kind words with her, that week follows week almost without his talking to her, that he is always exhausted, and that he is not aware of his brusque and distant behavior towards her. Although he has always been that way, it is time to change, because what he has is not a marriage, a relationship, or anything similar. In the interview, I realize that he is truly a good man, but he is extraordinarily alexithymic, unable to express feelings. When one spouse suffers from this affliction, the other experiences great suffering. In explaining his childhood and teenage years, he says, "At home, I always heard that men controlled their feelings and that expressing them was effeminate therefore, men should keep them under wraps."

He says, "She already told me a few weeks ago, very ceremoniously, that she wanted to talk to me; I thought that she needed more allowance or that there was some problem with one of the children at school. I was shocked with this proposal to separate. She's known how I am since we started dating each other; there were no surprises. Now, you tell me that this character of mine makes marriage very difficult, that I need to think about it, and see what you advise me to do. I married for life; for me divorce would be a big failure. What should I do and how do I do it? I am going to put total dedication into saving this marriage; although for me, things are not as bad as my wife makes them out to be."

In this case, he shows two especially negative features. The first is alexithymia, the incapacity to express feelings, which is a deep emotional deficit, manifested in both verbal nonverbal communication, such as gestures, facial expressions, and body movement.[3] There is a relationship between this affliction and depressive states,[4] more precisely a depressive personality. When present in married life, it can cause strong emotional pain. These individuals are emotionally illiterate. They do not know that married love needs words and gestures to survive and grow; if either disappear or have never been present, maintaining a healthy relationship is very difficult. The second feature is work addiction, which is common today. Many people live for work. They focus exclusively on their professional lives and invest less and less time in their spouses and children.

We created two individualized behavioral patterns with specific areas for improvement, which had positive effects in the weeks that followed.

In his case, the main objectives were:

1. I must learn strategies to express feelings more often and better (quantity and quality).
2. I must work less and come back home earlier to spend more time with my wife and children.
3. I must invest more time in my wife. We must share more things, both the two of us alone and with close friends.

---

3. It is a lack of color in our emotional relationship with others. If not corrected, it drives marriage into a stagnating and insufferable condition. Over ninety percent of alexithymics are male, and they are usually unaware of their condition. The role of the psychologist or psychiatrist is to inform the patient of their condition and offer them behavioral patterns to correct it. In our case, the prognosis was good, thanks to the patient's good disposition and his willpower. Similarly, our team manifested an enormous motivation to help him; to motivate is to encourage for the better.

4. This is a pessimistic approach to life. Since people are conscious of their own style, it is normal to focus mainly on the negative traits of personality rather than on the good. It is commonly accompanied by an evident problem in the ability to express ideas verbally; they talk just enough, or less than enough.

5. I must avoid becoming affectionate only a few minutes before bedtime.

6. I must pay more attention to my nonverbal cues; more specific suggestions were offered.

7. I must become more involved in my children's lives, not only regarding school, but also their friends, hobbies, worries, and so on.

In her case, the instructions were:

1. I must be patient with my husband's progress.

2. I must value his effort.

3. I must give him positive stimuli, such as telling him that he is doing better and that he is on the right path.

4. I must help him to work less. Because this is chronic, I must talk with his colleagues about the change he is undergoing.

The case has taken a noteworthy turn for the better and today the couple is doing well.

Differences in spiritual beliefs

Now, we refer to two people, who started going out together when he was thirty-seven and she was thirty-one. They both come from the same city. He is a foreign languages teacher of English and French, and also owns a successful language school. She studied humanities and is currently unemployed, although she has taught humanities subjects in two schools.

She says, "We saw each other for a year; the relationship grew progressively because at first I was not sure. My family is deeply religious; my parents taught catechism and they volunteered in the parish. For them, spiritual life has always been essential. My mother has always taken the lead in the family in this sense; I have three siblings. I met this man one summer, at a friend's house. The subject of religion soon emerged; he told me that he believed in a superior being but not in the Church, and that no one could tell him what to do or what to believe. We talked about many things and soon became friends, although we were always having one disagreement or another. Sometimes, we spoke in English, a language in which I need to improve. They are both native speakers of Spanish. When my parents learned that I was going out with him and that he was not a believer, they were very upset by his religious indifference. My father wanted to meet him, but my mother did not. After several months, he came to our house a few times and there was a lot of tension between him and my parents. He insisted on having sex, as though it were the most casual thing in the world; at first I resisted, but I finally gave in. The relationship was good and bad at the same time."

He now tells us, "In my opinion, this debate between us is fictitious; the important thing is for two people to love each other, which we did. The rest is irrelevant.[5] I went to a religious school until I was fourteen, and then moved to a state-run secular school. I have always believed that there is too much pressure on this subject, as though they want to choose your path for you, and I've always resisted. In my opinion, her parents have done her more harm than good with her education, especially regarding religion, specifically when it comes to sex and religious practice. As I see it, the best religion is to behave honestly. The rest is superfluous."[6]

---

5. This is a very superficial remark, since married life is marked by multiple factors and it is wise to consider them all. Life is long and a married relationship can become very complex. Love is not enough for a good relationship; there are many more factors.

6. This person is right in some things, but he lacks education. Doing good is a very admirable principle, but we cannot leave it at that; we must dig deeper.

After many family tensions, he convinced her to go and live together; if all worked out well, they would get married later. Her parents were devastated; their relationship with their daughter waned; their relationship with him disappeared altogether. She found a job in a school, although it was not what she wanted to do; she worked there without much motivation. A year later, they got married at the registry office. Her parents didn't attend the wedding.

She explains, "Because I loved my husband, I had to end my religious practice. He convinced me that it was alright and that only love mattered. In fact, he said, 'I have several friends, who aren't believers and live together; everything is working fine with them.' I must admit that this lapse in my spiritual life has left me very empty. In addition, it has been hard to lose the closeness I had with my parents and siblings. We see each other every now and then. We had our first child and my husband told me, 'If you want to baptize him, I accept it, but I don't believe much in that.' We baptized him. A couple of years later, our second child came; he also accepted that baptism. The problem came later, when I wanted to send them to a religious school and he said no. He claimed that he had yielded enough and we had to send them to a school, which taught the essential subjects and languages; those were the really important things for their future."

She proceeds, "We had lots of arguments and tense moments. He is always verbally attacking my family, insults them constantly, and says that my education was repressive.[7] I have suffered a lot. His character is strong, imposing, and he's become used to my

---

7. This word was coined by Freud; when inappropriately used, it can cause great harm. The important thing is not to repress or stop anything, but to channel it in the best way possible. For example, we must not talk about sexual repression but of positive emotional-sexual education. This topic is rich in subtleties, which are beyond the scope of this book.

always yielding. I admit that my personality is diminished. We have been married for four years now; not long ago, I asked him to marry me in the Church. At first, he didn't want to, then he said that he didn't care, and finally he accepted. . . . Both sets of parents attended, but everything was very tense. After five years, I have concluded that our relationship is broken. I want to separate; I no longer love him. I don't see him in the same way, and I don't admire him anymore. I'm very depressed. I see more clearly that I shouldn't have married him. My lack of criteria and my tendency to yield all the time have put me in this position."

This is a clear case of how differences regarding the ultimate meaning of life can become a decisive problem. At first, these differences may look unimportant, but in the long run they may be unsolvable. As I have said elsewhere in this book, shared beliefs make couples more solid.[8]

As the husband in the last case says, if neither has solid beliefs and all they share is a set of very general ideas without the depth of a spiritual commitment, the couple will not discuss important questions. If further along a problem arises, they will do what they can to solve it; if they cannot, they will separate. Having a solid spiritual side requires sharing a faith, a set of principles; if lived coherently, this will provide a couple with enormous stability. I believe that this case is very representative.

---

8. See the section on "Common Beliefs," in chapter 6.

CHAPTER 8.

Pornography, the Debasement of Love

A Worldwide Epidemic

The percentage of youngsters in the civilized world viewing pornography is not known for sure; there is no question that its usage is widespread. Statistical studies abound, which face us with this reality. Some young people admit to its casual use; others consult with us because they are not able to talk about it with others.

Pornography was born as an industry in the United States and extended gradually to other regions. It is the new global scourge, a destructive and incontrollable plague. Many believe that this topic is a problem for a few bored youngsters, but the reality is that pornography is an epidemic. It spews forth from the internet, mobile apps, videos, and photos; it now seems that the sexual education of children between ten and twelve years old is in the hands of pornographers. It continues with adolescents becoming addicted, later, it remains with those caught in this trap for years.

The debate in the US during the early 1970s, when the commercialization of pornography was escalating, focused on the propagation of previously clandestine activities. Before the digital era, there were "adult" cinemas, pornographic magazines, and other materials, but these products were not easily available, especially to children. With the advent of the distribution of pornography via the internet, social media, and mobile apps, that limitation has now largely disappeared. We are facing a global phenomenon of massive proportions.

I met a young man of twenty, who was sent to me by his mother; she told me that she did not understand what happened to her son, who was a reader of books. She thought he had anxiety or a type of obsession. This man, a university student, confessed, "For three years, I have been addicted to pornography. I spend hours every day watching porn. In the beginning, I thought it was normal; all my friends viewed porn, but my case is terrible. . . . I don't feel well at all, please help me out."

A thirty-year-old psychiatrist, a member of my team, told me, "Doctor Rojas, you are making an error when you ask young patients if they view pornography. The question has to be formulated differently—'How much porn do you see?'—because they all see pornography."

Why Is Pornography Bad?

This question is fundamental; however, many do not seem to find it important. The answer is that it degrades the human being, converting the user into someone seeing women only as a sexual being. Pornography is a lie about sex. It offers an image of sex, which is unreal, delirious, and absurd; it becomes an obsession with an intensity linked to the level of consumption. Its consumers are people, who are physically and psychologically mature, with an intellect, sentiments, and healthy aspirations; however, their desire for authentic love, reasonable happiness, and an adequate family will be rendered more difficult by their addiction to porn. When a person becomes focused on sexual consumption, it is nearly a psychological rule that pornography tends to be addictive. We know today from serious studies that porn addiction is more serious than cocaine addiction, because it affects more complex brain connections.[1] It involves dependence, which is the tendency to search for it within a certain period of hours or days, along with tolerance, which requires more complex and new ingredients over time to achieve excitation. The addiction, which depends on frequency and intensity, is different for someone consuming sporadically than for someone with regular consumption, who becomes a real addict. It should be noted that many such addicts do not accept their state; they say that many people they know think the same.

We also need to pay attention to the women, who are victims of this pornographic work. Many of them suffer from sexual trafficking. Many are poor and uneducated, are used from a young age, and end up as prostitutes. It's a sordid and humiliating world.

Pornography Changes the Image of Woman

When asking young men consuming pornography what image they have of woman, in many cases they have trouble answering. When they do, we often hear: "For me, getting to know a girl means possibly having sex with her." "For me, pornography is important because it has helped me understand what sex is and how to enjoy it." "It does not make sense to marry and have children. This is a burden. For me, sex is to enjoy without problems." "Porn is great because you learn a lot."

---

1. A pioneer in this work is Patrick Carnes. See, for example, Patrick Carnes, *Don't Call It Love: Recovery from Sexual Addiction* (New York: Bantam Books, 1990).

Others, more conscious of their addiction, see it differently. They say, "Porn can be good at the start, to understand sex, but the problem is that it is addictive and becomes obsessive." "The problem is that it changes your version of women and you don't see love." "We all want to understand sex, but porn makes you less sensitive." "Without control, porn deforms you." "To see sex online kills your spiritual dimension."

It is interesting to see the statements of parents bringing their children to my clinic, after discovering they consume pornography. Their kids have generally played it down, felt humiliated, or highlighted that "all their friends do the same, this is normal." I have also heard the following phrases from parents. "I would never have expected this from my child; I am depressed," said a mother. "I imagined something, but I did not expect it to be that serious." "It has been a deception for us as parents, after the education we have given them." "Doctor Rojas, please take him out of this; my kid has been degraded." "We have seen the computer of our child. We have failed as parents." "It should be forbidden, or something should be done, because this destroys youngsters from within." "In this way, love and romanticism are lost. . . . Everything is brutal." A mother asked me, crying, "What will happen to my child, if he is lost in this slime and we don't cure him?"

Recurrent users of porn, failing to admit they are addicts, believe that in sex everything is possible and that you have to be daring, going as far as possible in your fantasies or possibilities. It has been demonstrated that this leads to dysfunctional sexual behavior. The effect for some women will be merely to think they need to be sexier to attract men; however, the focus on a perfect, sculptural body can lead to conditions in weaker women such as anorexia-bulimia, esthetical obsessions, and inferiority complexes. Youngsters seeing porn want to practice sex.

They want to do what they see. This leads to sexual aggression in schools and mistreatment of girls by boys. It is not surprising that it leads to teenage pregnancy and abortion. Pornography is a real master in selfishness, where one thinks only of oneself. Experts say that pornography is about five A's: affordable, accessible, anonymous, accepted, and aggressive.

The Influence of Pornography on Married Men

Pornography and masturbation form an inseparable pair. For an already married person, who has been a frequent, usual, or addictive consumer, the sexual relation with himself lasts a few minutes until reaching pleasure. He then remains satisfied. But when this person has relations with his wife, who ignores or plays down the fact that her husband watches pornographic images, she is the one who suffers while her husband tries to replicate a fantasy. This can lead to her estrangement, and eventual separation. The American Psychological Association in many recent scientific editorials and surveys, has brought out the negative consequences of the sexualization of women as objects of pleasure. It prevents recognition of the rich range of possibilities women have, leaving only pleasure, emotion, and novelty.

Clinical case: how pornography affects conjugal life

A couple comes to the clinic. They have been married for seventeen years. He is forty-seven years old and works in financial investments. She is forty-two years old and works in a school as a history and literature teacher. They have three children, who are sixteen, thirteen, and nine years old. The wife made the first appointment and came to the clinic without her husband to explain the following:

"Until three years ago, my marriage has more or less worked well, with typical things that happen in any marriage. I have been realizing for a while that my husband consumes pornography. At the beginning, I was surprised; I thought it was something accidental, which occurred one night when he stayed working while I was sleeping. I woke up at dawn to go to the bathroom and entered the room where he worked. I was shocked. . . . He told me that he was using his computer and those images appeared. Since then, I have found more evidence of his use of porn. . . . I have searched his mobile phone and computer; the matter is serious."

While crying and regretting not having taken action sooner, she explains, "At the beginning he denied it, then said it was occasional, and little by little he has been accepting that it is an addiction. . . . He has disappointed me. I no longer admire him and he has become vulgar for me. We had strong arguments, and recently I have threatened to leave him. Our children two daughters and one son, are now aware of this problem and they are also very surprised."

After a few days, both came to the clinic, without his knowing that his wife had already spoken to me. He entered first and told me, "I didn't want to come to see a psychiatrist because I do not think that I need one, but my wife insisted. Our relationship as a couple is now complicated, but I think this is normal in any relation; my wife is exhausted, spends many hours at school where she works a lot; our two daughters are in full adolescence. I have probably been too cold with her. For me all of this is more or less normal."

He did not tell me, anything about pornography, which surprised me. I asked him, "Is there anything else that is relevant, that you haven't told me?" He answered, "Well, yes, my wife has caught me sometimes watching pornography and she has been very angry with me. She said for her this is like an infidelity." I asked, "How often do you view pornography?" He answered, "I don't know, occasionally, in my free time. Many friends my age tell me that they do too." I pressed him, "How often do you view it?" He told me, "A few times a week, when I am relaxed, on weekends."

I left him doing a series of psychological tests, regarding personality, state of mood, marital relations, and so forth. I asked him to leave in writing the following information:

- Main areas of conflict between my wife and myself, classified from most to least important.
- What would I change to improve our marital relation?
- The same but for my wife.
- Do you think pornography is bad? And if so, why?
- Additional information, such as important things that we had not discussed in our clinical interview.

Then, the wife proceeded to speak with me, and I told her that her husband had not openly spoken about pornography. She insisted that this was key for her and told me, "If he does not stop, I will separate from him."

We started a therapy, principally with him, about pornography. I told him, "You have to know that being a more or less frequent consumer of pornography, which he minimized while his wife maximized it, represents for any woman a rejection. I am going to give you some psychological strategies to fight this. Because of this addiction, your marriage could end. For your wife, this is now the most important thing. If you are not able to solve this, your relationship with her will be difficult."

In the following visits, I noticed that he was a good professional in his job but affectively immature. We designed a conjugal therapy program for each of them, separately, taking into account that he needed more help than his wife. I want to highlight two of the psychological guidelines we gave her: knowing how to evaluate the psychological progress of her husband and not speaking about pornography with him. I asked her to leave this in our hands.

The evolution has been positive. He told me, "This topic of pornography has been difficult for me because I saw it as a hobby, as a curiosity, but now I recognize that I was addicted. I see that it was detrimental to my relationship with my wife."

This clinical example is representative of what I have been saying. The physical and psychological wounds of pornography in family life are very destructive and it takes time to cure them. The main effects are that the woman stops admiring the man, who falls into this trap. Trust is lost. The man lies or falsifies reality. At the same time, the sexual relation of the couple deteriorates, because the woman realizes that her partner asks her for strange, new, and unhealthy conduct in what should be a relationship of love and generosity. The physical and psychological beauty of woman is lost. She is downgraded. Conjugal crisis and breakup are the fate for many of these couples.

Pornography among Adults

The addiction to pornography has turned into a worldwide epidemic. Recently, a huge child pornography and homosexual network was discovered in some countries of the European Union. Pornography destroys marriages, families, and the lives of people caught in this trap. Two recent books reveal the nature of the crisis: one from Peter Kleponis, an American psychologist, entitled *Pornography: Understanding and Confronting the Problem*; and another from Óscar Tokumura, who analyzes online pornography.[2] There is big business behind this scourge, which enslaves and destroys its consumers.

Millions of children and preadolescents are addicted to pornography. This changes their vision of women, love, intimate relations, and the real meaning of a healthy sexual relationship. Nobody talks about this. What are the main repercussions of pornography at these ages? Firstly, it is an abrupt introduction to sexuality, with no adequate explanation from the parents.

Sexuality is a language of committed love. It is a great symphony, which includes our physical, psychological, spiritual, and biographical components separately and jointly. Sex goes from being a body-to-body relation, sporadic and superficial, to a person-to-person relation, a deep and solemn encounter full of meaning. The key is to integrate sexuality in the couple's common project and do it harmoniously. Intimate relations have a key function in conjugal life, of total gift of self. Pornography severely damages this function; it is therefore no surprise that it plays an important role in seventy percent of divorces.

---

2. Peter C. Kleponis, *Pornografía: comprender y afrontar el problema* (Madrid: Voz de Papel, 2018); Óscar Tokumura, *La pornografía on line* (Barcelona: Los Libres, 2017). Kleponis has published similar books in English: see *Restoring Trust: A Couple's Guide to Getting Past Porn* (Huntingdon, Ind.: Our Sunday Visitor, 2018).

CHAPTER 9.

Some Behavioral Hints for Solving Marital Conflicts

Basic Ideas

Drawing on previous chapters, I will summarize some basic ideas to be applied in a conflict situation. Two ideas form a sequence: first, falling in love, and second, staying in love. Falling in love is escaping our own personal prison and needing the other person's happiness for our own well-being. This is why falling in love is a form of enthusiasm, a word deriving from the Greek *enthusiasmós,* which means to be full of God. It is a double happiness, which projects from us first and later bounces back onto us. The keys required to remain in love are admiration[1] and respect, which means valuing the other for their coherence and biography and always treating each other well and with dignity. There are a lot of elements at work in this definition, so I will rephrase as follows: staying in love is a polygon of infinite sides, the most important of which are

---

1. Falling in love is an emotion; love is a feeling. The former is intense and passionate; the second is more serene and rational. We must learn to combine them. This is what emotional maturity means. Admiration says that the person we have found is valuable and handbook of virtues for life. In order to admire someone, we have to be good ourselves and we have to follow their trajectory with attention.

the already mentioned admiration and respect, along with spirituality,[2] complementarity, and the willingness to carry out a common project.

We have reviewed the seven ingredients of lasting love. We cannot allow technological, scientific, political, informational, and social advances to obscure such a decisive dimension of life, true love. This book can provide the reader with solid pillars and stable foundations, useful for maintaining a happy, serene, and hopeful marriage, capable of overcoming problems and of approaching them with a positive attitude. In *The Everlasting Man,* G. K. Chesterton says that reality must be contemplated from a distance, because if we analyze any important event from too close, we lack perspective and vision. This is what I have tried to do in this book. Love embraces all dimensions of the person. Having a clear concept of this important issue is so fundamental. We must allow our minds to lead our hearts, showing them the way but without destroying love's vitality, dynamism, and freshness. This is the role of intelligence over will. A disoriented love will have severe consequences, which will become worse with the passing of the years. The lack of criteria will confuse us amidst the bombardment of ideas, so prevalent in this relativist and permissive society. Consequently, a correct learning of feelings is an important subject in our education.[3]

Human beings are born to love and be loved. Intelligence and will must shape and educate feelings with firmness and

---

2. Spirituality is the fine-tuning of our soul for immaterial things. Religiosity derives from it, and it implies a code of conduct and a religious practice. The three monotheist religions are all capable of giving an answer to true love, but the Judeo-Christian tradition offers the best version. When love has a strong and coherent spirituality, it has no expiration date.

3. Emotional education should be taught at school; it is not a marginal issue.

gentleness; I have said so throughout these pages. Such emotional intelligence is an art. It does not appear of its own accord; rather it must be the consequence of education. Feelings must be ordered so the best results can be obtained; this applies to parental love and to tenderness between spouses. We must be thankful and learn to apologize whenever necessary. Intelligence and will regulate and channel feelings. Emotional maturity is a result of the harmonious development of the person in all dimensions, not just one or two.

Let us revisit some of these patterns of conduct that we have examined.

Ability to forgive

Forgiveness is a great act of love. Here I am referring to forgiveness in cases where a great offense has been inflicted through words, actions, or omissions. We must learn to forgive in this hardened society. Where there has been physical or psychological abuse, forgiveness is difficult. The range of sufferings potentially experienced is very broad. It forms a diverse mosaic of disappointment, sadness, and hopelessness. Everything can be forgiven, if the will exists to start anew. Suffering may become so unbearable that a couple sees separation as the only way out, but before reaching such a drastic decision, we should exhaust all the means at our disposal in trying to avoid it.[4] At the opposite end, stands forgiveness. This has a twofold manifestation. The first is immediate, wherein mutual forgiveness is expressed, which is difficult; the second is long-term, which takes time and which consists of giving up hatred and vengeance, trying to forget our

---

4. In such a divorcist society as ours, such advice may sound strange. To make the greatest effort to solve problems is something wonderful, marvelous, extraordinary, and full of generosity. Forgiveness opens the door to the possibility of repair.

wounds. The best version of human greatness is thus manifested; we must renounce our wish to seek revenge, to correct, to apply the *lex talionis*, which can only be done by a superior human being.

Forgiving requires being able to forget what has happened and to consider the other as someone worthy of compassion, even if the offense inflicted is severe. Forgiveness is not possible without a profound sense of spirituality. However, we must be realistic; today the constant invitations to divorce may make all this sound strange and cause the reader to think that the author is asking for heroic feats. While there is some truth there, virtue is an aspiration to excellence; the best is easy to admire, but difficult to achieve. According to German philosopher Jutta Burggraf, "Any pain that is simply denied and covered up returns through the back door and stays with us for a long time as a traumatic experience. Such wounds can cause permanent injury and even momentous delusions."[5] The act of forgiveness shows a superior wisdom. This will be better appreciated with the perspective of time. Vengeance and hatred poison life. Resentment is like an intoxication, which can become an obsession. The negative experiences of our past will thus be hard, heavy, devastating in our minds, and causing a deflagration of revenge against the person who did us ill.

The ability to forget and forgive is a feature of emotional maturity and love. In this case, the losers end up as the winners. A psychologically healthy person lives in the present, fights with all their might to get over past grievances, and works for a future full of hope. We can also put it the other way around; those trapped by past traumas and incapable of putting distance between themselves and that pain will become what

---

5. Jutta Burggraf, *Learn to Forgive* [Spanish: *Aprender a perdonar.* https:// es.catholic.net/op/articulos/10021/cat/829/aprender-a-perdonar.html#modal]

classic psychiatry called neurotic.[6] Forgiveness is not creating a clean slate, as though nothing had happened. True forgiveness is renouncing vengeance and hatred for a superior end. I forgive, I fight to forget, I don't keep accounts of the wounds received, and I grow to face adversity. I know that this sounds heroic, but it is the pirouette of excellence and the fine wine of superior wisdom. The first challenge that I suggest is being able to forgive everyone and everything, which is superhuman.

It is obvious that such a demanding task, such a psychological feat, does not preclude justice. There is neither justice without forgiveness, nor forgiveness without mercy. Forgiveness is the way forward in marriage and the system to undo knots. Mercy is superior to justice.

Do not bring up past grievances

This is a very healthy attitude and another cornerstone for intelligent love. The list of grievances is that inventory of mistakes, shortcomings, and wrongdoings, big or small, which have occurred during life in common. In bad moments, this list is always ready to emerge and be heard. Its effects can be devastating and even demolishing. It is bringing back over and over again all that has been bad.

Very often this catalogue of reproaches and criticism emerges with force; my personal experience has shown me that the habit of bringing up the past can be the cause of the end of a marriage, if not corrected in time. It makes dialogue more difficult, because it is an invasive wish to relive all those bad experiences. When psychologists and psychiatrists begin therapy with a couple, one

6. This word has seeped into everyday language and means a badly adjusted person, a person with open wounds, with unresolved conflicts, and very prone to aggression or anxiety.

of their most important roles must be helping them avoid such behavior. I want to give four weighty arguments as to why it is not a good idea to keep this list of grievances:

1. It is not constructive. It does not help progress. Exhibiting our list of complaints is toxic and, if not kept under control, causes irreparable damage.

2. It makes reliving the past a recurrent pattern, preventing us from advancing forward.

3. It causes neurosis; it makes people tense, bitter, wounded, and full of unresolved conflicts.

4. It can influence future relationships, since people can have severe difficulties in overcoming their negative past.

Avoid unnecessary discussions

Well-oiled couples have very few arguments. They have learned that arguments neither reveal truth nor create harmony. For this reason, they can be silent when the situation demands it; they can control themselves. Psychologists and psychiatrists stress this point constantly during couples therapy.[7] We must distinguish between dialogue, differences of opinion, and discussions:

---

7. Some experts highlight the importance of not arguing or keeping it to a minimum. Three useful works are: Aaron Beck, *Love is Never Enough,* cited in chapter 1. Beck is a professor of psychiatry in New York; the book is full of good suggestions, developed after a long career working with troubled couples; Paul Hauck, *Making Marriage Work* (London: Sheldon Press, 1977), which is a compilation of easy case studies useful for learning how to correct common mistakes; and Luis Rojas Marcos, *La pareja rota* (Madrid: Espasa Calpe, 2003), which offers a clear and dynamic perspective on how to avoid reaching the point of no return.

Current literature on couples therapy is very extensive; divorce has become an epidemic and there are many people trying to find solutions to their marital problems.

- *Dialogue* means talking, exchanging opinions and experiences on the most diverse topics. It teaches how to listen and how to produce logical arguments.
- Differences of opinion indicate different points of view on reality, helping us to grow and improve our ideas and beliefs, as well as to clearly explain our own opinions. A true friend, while having different opinions from us, respects us and shows us another perspective on reality.
- Arguments, are more like disorganized debate; they stem from a clear disagreement, and they can degenerate into a hard, bitter, sharp exchange in which we aim more to score points against our spouse than to find the truth.

Learning not to have arguments is very beneficial for a couple. In my experience as a psychiatrist, I have been witness to true dialectic battles full of mutual accusations. So-called misunderstandings must be sorted out with serene words and a common will to yield.

The most balanced member of the couple will have to cut the argument short and direct the conversation to other topics. For obsessive individuals, this diversion becomes a serious problem.

Learn to value things within family life at their true worth

Sound judgment is knowing how to value things at their true worth, not turning any menial problem into a drama, and having a long-term vision.[8] Knowing how to differentiate the accessory from the necessary and a mere anecdote from what is truly important, are clear signs of a maturity. This is an art. It translates

---

8. Long-term vision is a way of looking at things with greater perspective, which shows a superior intelligence, as opposed to short-term vision, observing things only through a perspective of immediacy. The first must form a part of the mechanics of married life.

into balance and self-control. Avoiding dramatizing situations gives us moderation, judgment to evaluate circumstances, and strength to resist being swept away by difficulties.

Therefore, before any problem or conflict may appear, our first reaction must be a serene evaluation of the facts, wherein we avoid rushing into action, anxiety, uncontrolled impulses, or loss of self-control. It does not mean doing nothing and waiting for the problem to vanish. We must confront conflicts with a clear head, measuring all available solutions. Looking to sensible people around us for advice is often a very sound decision. The lack of a measured consideration will lead to hasty and passionate actions.

Respect each other

Mutual respect is a very important factor. What should we do when the attitude of our spouse becomes unbearable or unnerving, with no apparent way to correct it? The solution is to talk about it with diplomacy and delicacy but also with firmness. In these cases, we must learn to focus on the specific topic under discussion, without adding negative events from the past. This takes discipline. It is the only way to reach agreements and find solutions. If this person is not capable of changing after being asked several times, the best thing is to accept it with love and elegance, without becoming obsessed, remembering that we all have stolid and unmovable traits of behavior. We must not dramatize the issue.

Respect consists of words, gestures, and actions. They are all related to one another. An inappropriate use of harsh words and reproachful expressions is very negative. We must also avoid excessive and unfortunate corrections, such as, "You talked too much during that dinner party," "You drank too much," "You told this story but that's not how it really happened," and the like. There is a type of controlling person, who is obsessed with his or her spouse or partner being perfect or almost so. These people have become used to correcting the other in everyday life, both when they are alone and in the company of others. This demonstrates poor marital dexterity. Many who suffer from this problem are not aware of it or they see it, as normal without realizing how much damage it can cause.

Similar gestures would be grimaces, angry and disapproving expressions, and so on. As I have stated throughout this book, good nonverbal communication facilitates cooperation and emotional intelligence.

Learn to get over bad days or conflicts

Couples must know that these things happen, because married life experiences a multitude of different circumstances. It is easy for life in common to produce misunderstandings and small problems; they are part of the script. The important thing is for the most generous of the two to ask for forgiveness at once. Afterwards, this must be followed by positive gestures, such as a kiss, a hug, or some little detail, and the will to forget everything and never go back to it again.

Hypersensitive people are often embittered by the memory of these past events, making the smooth function of life in common difficult. We must learn not to exaggerate such experiences and to understand that they are normal in married life.

Learn communication skills

Nowadays, this is called assertiveness, which is knowing how to go through life sorting out difficulties and avoiding committing gross mistakes in our life in common. This issue embraces multiple factors, including tact and diplomacy to explain what displeases us; the ability to choose the right moment to do so; the skill to put things mildly and not to be too direct in our opinion of the other; and the ability to laugh at ourselves and to avoid arguments when there is a difference of opinion. We must realize that having different opinions is normal and good; it is very rare for both spouses to coincide 100 percent in everything.

Find more humor in everyday life

For some couples, the smallest thing becomes a big problem. These couples radically exaggerate details and take events out of their original contexts; they live life like a soap opera or a Greek tragedy, making life in common an unbearable experience. Others tend to always see the negative side of things, to anticipate bad outcomes even before they occur, and always assume the worst. We must learn to do things the other way around.

Having a sense of humor is an exclusive feature of intelligent people. Cultivating it helps us see the enjoyable in the mundane. It is smiling, being ironic, taking things with a grain of salt, and filing away life's sharp edges. These are strategies to fight hopelessness. A couple sharing a developed sense of humor will attain a good degree of unity, and they will have the resources needed to confront adversity and avoid argument.

Never talk about divorce

This is one of the most common mistakes in marriages. "We will separate, if things continue like this"; "I will leave you any day now"; and "If things continue like this, I will go and see a lawyer to sort things out and we can go different ways."

In discussions and debates within a marriage, these ideas are often brandished, sometimes as a threat, sometimes as blackmail, and sometimes as a mantra having become difficult to control. They wear the relationship out and make us consider a possibility, which encourages us to give up fighting to correct our defects.

There is no benefit to talking about divorce, so it should never be mentioned. And when I say never, I mean never.

Look after your intimate life with zeal

Sex is important, but not the most important thing; it should be given its right place at all times. Couples should talk about it to avoid the estrangement resulting from lack of communication. Giving ourselves sexually involves a rich psychological exchange, and it should focus on ensuring the satisfaction of the other. Sexual life within a married couple is a game of generosity.

Avoid distortions in your perception of reality

Everything has a subjective dimension. Our perception is inevitably colored by our own bias. In couples going through difficulties, the same fact can be interpreted very differently, causing strong confrontations. Difficult cases would do well in looking for a referee, somebody close and accepted by both, to grant some peace and try to find solutions. The true friend plays a very important role here, and his or her intervention can have very positive results. Friends must come from both sides of the couple. Friends enrich our life and must be looked after. Friendship is affinity, generosity, and intimacy. Having a few intimate friends is a treasure; they are not easy to find, but when we do our personal life expands and fills with new potential.

Stop your tendency to control, monitor, and spy on your spouse

In my personal experience, this tendency is more common in women than in men. I am not a sexist person; I admire modern women, who have had to prove much more than men to reach similar levels of professional consideration, but I have seen many controlling women, who monitor and inspect their husbands' conduct, quick to criticize it. When this becomes a recurrent feature, the other person enters a wearisome state of despondency. As so often happens with small or medium-sized defects in life in common, these people are not usually aware of the problem, or at least of its frequency; becomes essential for their spouses to approach it with diplomacy. Learning to talk about difficulties in our relationship is an art, which takes time and skill. We have to go about it, little by little; if the effort is made from early on, the long-term consequences are very positive.

Always have spiritual reasons for overcoming difficulties, problems, life-changing moments, and unexpected circumstances

I direct the reader once again to the section about common beliefs. There we discuss the different facets of the quintessence of love in detail, as a kind of hidden science hosting the *ars magna* of our love life, an essential ingredient of the alchemy of married love. A shared spirituality is the card up our sleeve; this card brings magic, secret codes, and a unity difficult to achieve otherwise. Christianity is a joyful, vital religion, which strengthens and encourages all facets of married life. If lived with coherence and realism, Christian principles are a considerable help for tackling all the difficulties that life may pose.[9]

An Ending that Is a Beginning

Dear reader, the book is drawing to an end. I hope that the ideas expressed in it are clear to you. I have worked on these ideas for

---

9. Our society needs more witnesses than instructors. Witnesses are examples of life, models to be followed. They offer tangible examples. Their strength is great. Here we can talk about learning by positive imitation.

many years, and I have tried to summarize them succinctly. I think that this final stage of our trip is a good moment for the design of a decalogue for a good life in common. I am offering ten suggestions to help your relationships to function. The task is not easy.

Commandments For Married Life

1. **Always be ready to give and to receive love.** This implies a permanent, two-way, emotional exchange. To love is to give ourselves to the other person, wishing the best for him or her. Goodness must be our aim, that which can satiate our deepest thirst. Goodness is our loftiest aspiration, wholeness, perfection. Every man and woman in love must aspire to the best, regardless of the inevitable difficulties, which life in common will bring.

   Giving and receiving love is an emotional exchange in which each reinforces the other through verbal gratification, positive communication patterns, good psychological interaction, rewards, instruments to make the other person feel loved, and many other methods.

   Love is the supreme act of freedom; nothing can fulfill human life more than having our hearts full of love. The best married relationships point to solidarity; this must be achieved through hard work.

2. **Bear in mind the importance of small things**, those little details that make life in common a pleasurable experience. This is often highlighted in various branches of modern operative psychology, behavioral, cognitive, and connectionist. Gottman and his collaborators have created the so-called "bank-account model" to refer to this exchange of positive

rewards.[10] Such behaviors are almost insignificant in and of themselves, but tending them or neglecting them can significantly influence our relationships for good or bad.

3. **Try not to be hypersensitive.** An excess of susceptibility can make life in common unbearable. Therefore, we must correct hypersensitivity, or having what is colloquially know as a "thin skin" and feeling wounded by insignificant details, before it affects the relationship. We must learn to guide our actions by our thoughts and not by our heart, however without becoming less human. Being rational is important, but not so much so that we lose touch with our emotions.

4. **Avoid unnecessary arguments.** The utmost effort must be invested here. It is rare that the truth comes as a consequence of arguments, because they usually serve as an exchange of frustrations. It is dangerous when a couple enters a dynamic of constant arguments, accusations, and verbal aggressions, because the harsh words they exchange in moments of carelessness leave an impression and are difficult to forget. They feed the so-called "list of grievances."

5. **If there is an argument, react quickly and deal with the negative situation** without letting it get worse. A couple must not go for hours or days without talking to each other. Negative gestures or secluded attitudes, which are worse still, even if less obvious, must also be avoided. An attitude of hypercritical interior language is called negative cognitive language. It is always useful to apologize, trying to practice

---

10. J. M. Gottman and L. J. Krokoff, "Marital Interaction and Satisfaction: A Longitudinal View," *Journal of Consulting and Clinical Psychology*, 57, no. 1, 1989, pp. 47–52; John Gottman and Nan Silver, *Seven Principles for Making Marriage Work* (London: Orion Books, 2007).

small strategies for reconciliation before the situation worsens. After a problem, diplomacy must be exercised to look for a solution in which the other does not feel defeated. It is especially helpful to reach small, constructive agreements.

6. **Be careful what your verbal and nonverbal language conveys,** always striving for respect, understanding, and diplomacy. In married life, words, gestures, and attitudes are equally important. Exercising good manners creates an environment in which everybody tries to improve themselves. Research into communication patterns between couples, both stable and unstable, observes that the latter often show discrepancies in symbolic interpretation.[11] Couples in conflict are prone to misunderstandings, communication failures, distortion of verbal and nonverbal messages, disagreements, poor listening skills, and limited empathy.

   For these reasons, couples therapy often focuses on teaching communication skills, specifically highlighting three important factors: respect, with which both explicitly recognize the other's dignity, demonstrating it through words, gestures and actions; understanding, which always implies getting into the other's shoes and thus changing the reference framework; and finally, diplomacy, which must not be neglected if the relationship is to keep its freshness. We must be attentive, affectionate, and generous.

7. **Avoid bringing up past grievances,** if you want to maintain the stability of your relationship. Sometimes couples are drawn into a tense situation because of some small incident

---

11. Ernest Porterfield, "Black-American Intermarriage in the United States," *Marriage and Family Review* 17, 1982; Kathryn D. Rettig and Margaret M. Bubolz, "Interpersonal Resource Exchanges as Indicators of Quality of Marriage," *Journal of Marriage and Family* 45, no. 3, 1983, pp. 497–509.

or as a result of tiredness. An Eastern legend says, "words are silver, and silence is golden." Learning to stay silent when appropriate is the best course of action; and it implies a great strength, controlling our tongues means controlling ourselves. In some couples, this has become almost impossible because insults and harsh words have already imposed themselves on the relationship. If such behaviors are not corrected in time, they could be the beginning of the end.

8. **Exercise good timing to bring up conflicts** or to make important decisions. This is tremendously important for a harmonious life in common; it is learned with training. Being able to communicate and choosing the right place and time is essential. It is also important to maintain a certain order in the issues discussed, not to plan to discuss them all at once, and, for example, to avoid discussing problems in the evening, when we are tired after work.

9. **Love is an exchange of rewards requiring training.** Throughout this book, I have insisted that love can be learned; this is why it is an art. Coordinating two lives is not easy; it is impossible without effort. The patterns for solid relationships develop in the equilibrium of gradually acquired mutual understanding, and it is important to introduce little surprises to break the monotony. It is essential for each couple to find its own magnetic fields, to create points of mutual attraction, and to put them to work.

Having a solid marriage for which we have worked, correcting what was failing, and adding what was lacking is one of the happiest experiences of life. It is the culmination of our personal project.

10. **Learn to listen.** Communication skills are essential for the stability of a relationship. Listening is a daily task, a set of lessons

to be learned in the right order: letting the other speak; listening attentively until he or she has finished; being mindful of volume and tone of voice in our comments and observations; always being respectful; avoiding insults and accusations; not seeking hidden meanings but rather limiting ourselves to what the other actually says; not being sarcastic, overcritical, or depreciative; being careful with interpretations of words, gestures, or attitudes; maintaining our attention on the topic at hand without leaping from one issue to another, leaving them all unresolved; asking our partner what concrete things we can change about ourselves to improve the relationship; and avoiding expressions like: "I can't stand you," "That's inadmissible," "This better be the last time," "I can't handle your attitude," or "You always want to be right."

Sharp expressions impede reconciliation. It is also important to bear in mind that some of the other person's negative traits are deeply ingrained and are therefore difficult to eradicate; in such cases, the best thing is to avoid talking about them, by dodging them while focusing on positive features. Let us not forget that married love is generosity and acceptance of the reality of the other.

Chapter 10

An End That Is a Beginning

1. It Takes Time to Arrive at Simplicity

Simplicity is the virtue of a mature individual. It lies in the art of reducing the complex down to the fundamental—to an indivisible form, which is easy to understand or do. The quality of simplicity is expressed in that which has neither artifice nor ostentation, which expresses that concept as it really is. Straightforwardness without duplicity. It is the most diaphanous of values: transparent, clear, without guile.

As a psychiatrist, I frequently see individuals who are mentally complicated, and sometimes I tell them, "Your worst enemy is your mind. It plays tricks on you, runs all over the place uncontrollably, and subjects you to ups and downs that cause worries, fears, bad omens, and negative anticipations."

I want to make a distinction between two contrasting meanings of the world *simple.* I will begin by addressing the first meaning of the word, where a "simple" person is an individual who deals with important matters in a vague, superficial manner, without giving them nuance or subjecting them to any serious analysis. In fact, we use the term in colloquial language, with some contempt, to say, for example, "That person is very simple," by which we mean that they are a simpleton. They lack seasoning or flavor; they are plain, dim, unqualified, and incapable of

159

intelligent conversation. On the contrary, the other meaning of *simple* refers to those who are not superficial, who lack ostentation, who are able to be themselves, and who aspire to a certain coherence of life where there is a good relationship present between what they say and what they do. Be what you are, without worrying about looking a certain way, without pretending. There aren't many virtues as pleasant as this: individuals with this good kind of simplicity are easy people to live with, easy to love, and it is easy to understand what they are thinking; they give complete and accurate answers that adjust to reality.

Going from person to concept, simplicity is *the ability to penetrate reality with fairness of judgement, looking for the essence of something*. It discerns what is substantial and irreducible. It is not stupidity, but an accurate, sharp, precise gaze that, knowing the complexity of everything, seeks out what is essential. Simplicity of thought means that we are not victims or prisoners of it: it is freedom, grace, clarity, luminosity. To bet on simplicity is to aspire to peace and serenity, to be uncomplicated, to seek what is clean and diaphanous. The water in a pond can appear deep if it is cloudy; offshore, in the Mediterranean, you can see the bottom, which appears to be so close we can almost touch it, when in reality it is many meters deep.

Mental simplicity is knowing what you want and having a clear hierarchy of values—and acting accordingly. Nothing more and nothing less. This means being present in reality. And for that it is good to lay hold of prudence: the Scholastics said that it is the garage where justice, fortitude, and temperance are kept. Prudence does not reign, but it governs.

Simplicity is learned little by little. It's a task of goldsmithing that pushes us toward reality in a sober manner. It's an atmosphere dotted with calmness, where peace and joy flash— a key binomial that sneaks into the individual and reaches the ins and outs that engineer behavior, producing a particularly pleasant state of mind. It's a life strewn with solid, strong, consistent arguments.

Simplicity is a virtue of children. Let's not forget that they are the ones who ask fundamental questions about life. Bare and direct. Their naivete and immediacy make them potential philosophers. My six-year-old grandson Jesus asks me, "Grandad, why do birds fly? Why do people get sick and fall ill? Why do people get sad and cry?"

Intelligence is the capacity to synthesize information, the knowledge of how to distinguish between fundamental elements, and the art of reducing the complex down to the simple. Spanish philosopher José Ortega y Gasset says that clarity is a courtesy. The opposite would be the cryptic and far-fetched, the twisted and crossed rhetoric that aims to reclaim the dark and enigmatic. It is a kind of affected opacity.

When faced with the complexity of so many issues, we must seek simplicity in everything—despite the complexity of thought, the simplicity of a glance. Simplicity is foreseeing and getting ahead with a calm evaluation of the present as well as a calm and effective approach to the future. In semantics, this word combines moderation, temperance, elegance, and sobriety of thought. It means to communicate many things with clarity and with very few words.

It takes time to arrive at simplicity. In the sphere of thinking, it is nothing more than the art of staying afloat in a sea of ideas, all of which jump, rise, fall, circulate, and run uncontrollably, often due to the excess of information to which we are subjected today. Simplicity of the mind is reflected through behavior. We know this as psychiatrists. In those with so-called personality disorders—who in German psychiatry of the mid-twentieth century were called neurotic individuals—according to the American Psychiatric Association, one of the most prominent features is to mentally complicate matters within the mind: intrusive, twisted, negative thoughts, in anticipation of the worst, in which a mosaic of ideas parade, presided over by anxiety and restlessness.

Nowadays we are subject to social media in a manner which I have called the *Syndrome of Information Excess*, even more so during the course of the pandemic that has surrounded us. It is easy to be swept away by a whirlwind of news into a jungle of facts and figures that dissolve in the Milky Way of everything that enters the mind. The media looks for novelties and surprises, an ongoing frenzy of news pieces that devour one another. This brings me to the distinction between *information* and *practice*. There are clear differences between them. Having *information* means being aware of what is happening around you. Having *practice* means knowing what to expect. It means having certain criteria to follow in order to manage your life as well as possible in the midst of the influx of news that often induces in us indifference and mediocrity due to the saturation of contradictions. We live in a society wounded by permissibility and petty theft and which is drugged by the media.

Simplicity is a virtue of the wise. That's why its effects lead to true psychological equilibrium, where all of the distinct parts of an individual are well-balanced. This attitude is full of moderation while being rich, expansive, and mature. Culture opens new horizons; wisdom opens new pathways. The first is horizontal and extensive, while the latter is vertical and intensive.

An eagle is made to fly and see life from a panoramic view. A human being with a good head on their shoulders has aquiline vision and the cunningness of a snake. Simplicity of thought is the heritage of the intelligent.

2. Who Would You Like to Look Like?

It is very important to have models of identity. Each one of us has to work on our personality with detail, in a handcrafted manner. When I was a young medical student, I had a very personal notebook, a list of people I wanted to be like. I said it in a very clear way: "When I am older, I want to be like . . ." I had a certain number of people who were my reference and whom I followed closely: my parents; Luis, my older brother; Sole, another of my siblings; and a few professors who were captivating. Then, as a doctor, I identified other people who had specific traits I admired: this one as an example of work; that one as an attractive personality; the other as exhibiting coherence of life.

A *model of identity* is an attractive human prototype that invites us to follow him, imitate him, and copy many features of his behavior. As a psychiatrist I appreciate the importance of this phenomenon and understand how to select such a model. I want to simplify this:

1. The process starts with finding someone special who catches our attention and who is a *living and open lesson,* with a message that pulls us in its direction.

2. The analysis of this person forms admiration and provokes a reaction within us to copy, to follow their footsteps, some steps more and some less. They are a reference, representing a notable archetype, a mirror to look into, an example of how to approach life, an ideal, a paradigm.

3. Everything follows a *gradual process of imitation*. It is rare that it is only incarnated in one person; normally we obtain it from specific facets of various people. From this person I adopt his integrity, from the other his dedication to the family, from yet another her professionalism or spirituality

or culture. This way I capture the best of people and try to put it into practice in my life.

4. When a person has had healthy, strong, positive, and attractive models of identity, which have worked like a magnet or call—everything becomes easier. It is the positive seduction, the esteemed reference. I want to take this path. I like this way of being and functioning. I want to make it mine.

5. There are two opposing learning processes: by *imitating* and by *contrast*. The first one is carried out by copying, imitating the positive things we discover in someone, the things that help me head in the right direction. The second goes the other way, doing the opposite of something negative that we see in our surroundings. A young boy says he learned from his father how *not* to treat a woman. Another says he learned from a politician how *not* to act when in charge of responsibilities. It is clear that the first, imitation, works better and has more accurate results.

6. *All learning is essentially cognitive.* This means that it develops through a process in which we absorb and store all the information from the outside that catches our attention and orders our mind. Once the information is in place, we will fly, discriminating and selecting what we think is best. The models of behavior and of life are transmitted through authentic lives that illuminate our future. Reason teaches us; actions convince us; exemplary lives draw us.

7. Nowadays, models of identity have diversified. At the same time it is modern means of communication that transmit some of them: the professional athlete, the singer, the politician. The problem is that many of them are copied without much discernment, without critically appraising them and with inadequate education. So we find ourselves

in the present culture: tattoos have become popularized; many imitate the life of famous people and separate themselves from their spouses over common difficulties of living together that could be solved with some effort; and other poor behaviors sneak into the lives of young people.

What is missing in our world are authentic models of identity from which we learn. They educate us, seduce us with goodness, and transport us toward the better. However, nowadays there are few leaders who produce admiration, who have the capacity to captivate and serve as guides. True leaders have authority: they help you to grow as a human being and furnish a reference that opens your horizons.

When you are young, you are full of opportunities; when you are older, you are full of realities. We are what we do, not what we say. That is why life is a result: it is the consequence of what I have done with it, in accordance with what I project. This is where two essential things arise: First, the need to work on my *personality* with dedication, smoothing the edges to make it more balanced, more mature, and more complete. Second, the need to start my coherent and realistic *project of life*, planned with my feet on the ground with the five major ingredients incorporated in it: love, work, culture, friendships, and hobbies.

Happiness consists of this: finding oneself and having a personal project of life. We seek it without forgetting that absolute happiness doesn't exist, and that we have to aspire to a *reasonable happiness*: a good relationship between what we have desired and what we have achieved. Don't ask of life what it cannot give us.

When a person has had strong and clear models of identity, the panorama of existence illuminates itself in an extraordinary manner. It is about following those steps. This way, one reaches a certain *plentitude*. Choosing good models of identity is key, and making a mistake in this is a grave error. Life is a hieroglyph that doesn't need to be deciphered.

3. Having Perspective

Life is the greatest teacher and experience the greatest mentor. Living is learning. Living is doing something worthwhile with your time, something positive, everyone according to their own possibilities and circumstances. The best thing is putting love and hope into the tasks you carry out. We live in a world that has perpetuated the *hic et nunc*—the here and now—or the so-called *hodie et nunc*—today and now. Both signify the culture of the moment or, in other words, the adoration of immediacy. Everything has become fast, dizzying, urgent. It is a kind of polymorphous cult of transience, glorifying the ephemeral. It is the urgent versus what can wait, the near versus the far.

In the course of my job, I am used to entering and leaving the lives of others with the intention of understanding what happens to them and getting to the bottom of their personality in search of the roots of their behavior. And then, implementing the means to help them get out of that adverse situation, whether they are depressive, anxious, uncertain, or fearful; when everything seems to be dark and gloomy, with no way out. But let's not dwell on the things that have already happened or that came out the opposite of what we expected: you have to be a bigger person than that.

This means that having a perspective on our personal life is crucial. We need to be able to have long-term vision of our biography, to observe from a distance by turning on the headlights. We must not dwell on negative experiences that have already happened but instead have the capacity to look forward to the horizon and discover that behind that failure, defeat, disappointment, shipwreck . . . we can find the good and the positive. This is the vantage point of experience that looks at things with a panoramic view. I have seen serious defeats that, after a relatively short time, have become an incentive that has served in advancing a person's life and the project that is each of us. Defeats turn into victories.

I have said many times in my books and in my articles that happiness and having a project of life form a binomial. We are talking about a mixture of emotional intelligence on the one hand and synthetic intelligence on the other. The first has been in fashion for some time now and we can define it as the ability to mix both the instruments of reason and the elements of the world of emotion. How can it be implemented in terms of perspective? By being able to look at the facts with a fresh pair of eyes and knowing that failures contain many hidden values within them: they make us humbler; they cure us of arrogance; they strengthen willpower; and they encourage us to fight and start over and to truly value what a small victory is.

Failure is a fundamental part of any life. By being free, we can fail, make mistakes, approach important issues in an inadequate way . . . but we are also free to correct ourselves, to progress, to realize the importance of those bad moments. Failure teaches what success is. These are lessons that cannot be learned from books.

In simple terms, having the courage and determination to overcome what goes wrong or differently than anticipated is one of the indicators of a strong individual. Things may affect us in the short-term, but in the long run they are of little significance. There are victories that are the result of losses. Many secrets of good lives lie in the fact that strong people who face adversities are capable of growing in the face of setbacks and misfortunes. Many are awakened by failure, while others are lulled by early success. To put it more expressively: those who lose, win. If we use our hearts and minds in unison, we are able to reinvent ourselves, to start over.

Synthetic intelligence is about the ability to summarize the facts and give concrete, precise information and, at the same time, test practical solutions to get back on track. It's about discovering where the root of failures lies, where we have gone wrong, how we can learn to have more realistic expectations, and how to better measure our goals on the one hand and our objectives on the other. For example, my goals are too general and broad and their outlines are imprecise; I want to be better, be more educated, improve professionally, have a healthier family life—all of these have a blurred, vague background. If goals are measured, we can track them quantitatively. If we are able to be clear about concepts, we will see real progress with our feet on the ground rather than daydreaming.

We are speaking, in short, of resilience—a concept that comes from physics and refers to the ability of certain metals to bend without breaking. It is the ability to cope with failures by encouraging improvement. Camilo José Cela once said, "He who resists wins."[1] Willpower also plays a role here, as a key piece in the organizational scheme of psychology: it means to endure and resist adversity with strength, with serenity, and the desire to overcome it. As a result, we become solid and strong, like the stones of a Romanesque or Gothic cathedral.

Happiness means overcoming. Unhappiness is like being in a basement with no view of the street. Happiness is fulfilment and forgetfulness, culmination and amnesia, and achievements that match expectations.

---

1. Camilo José Cela, "Prince of Asturias Award for Literature 1987," *https:// www.fpa.es/en/princess-of-asturias-awards/laureates/1987-camilo-jose-cela.html?text o=discurso&especifica=0.*

Index